TALES TO TELL MY DAUGHTERS

(as I Isolate During the COVID-19 Pandemic)

By T.R. Shand

A Golden Meteorite Press Book. Printed in Canada.

© Copyright 2020, T.R Shand, Austin Mardon, & Catherine Mardon.

Golden Meteorite Press, Edmonton. All rights reserved for Tales to Tell My Daughters©. No part of this publication may be reproduced, stored in any retrieval system, or transmitted in any form or by any means, electronic, mechanical, photocopying, recording, microfilm reproduction and copying, or, otherwise, without the prior express written permission of Golden Meteorite Press:

First Printing: 2020

Edited by Austin Mardon, Robbie Mcweeny & Riley Witiw
Design and Format by Kerstin Ekstrom

Telephone: 587-783-0059
Email: aamardon@yahoo.ca
Website: goldenmeteoritepress.com

Additional copies can be ordered from:
Suite 103 11919-82 Street NW
Edmonton AB T5B 2W4
CANADA

ISBN 978-1-77369-151-0

TALES TO TELL MY DAUGHTERS

(as I Isolate During the COVID-19 Pandemic)

By T.R. Shand

TABLE OF CONTENTS

Chapter 1	Life Before Children	15
Chapter 2	Married With Children	53
Chapter 3	Bonus Stories	83
Chapter 4	Golf Stories I Have Known	97

AUTHOR'S NOTES

Day 3: Look out for a book boom in the coming months. Many aspiring authors are taking this time to write. However, almost all will be self-published as few will interest publishers. I know not where my effort will land. But for those putting off writing for years, what better time than during the Coronavirus pandemic of 2020? (Wasn't Corona even the name of the old typewriter some of you have only seen in old B/W movies?)

Yes, I am one of those - an author in waiting. I actually had it in my (also unwritten) New Year's Resolutions for 2020. No, I did not resolve to be sent home for 14 days into self-isolation, but I did finally get started writing my book, for which all I had is the title "Tales to Tell My Daughters." Everything is pretty much a work in progress, as it very much depends on how things evolve in the next two weeks, less the two days since we were told to go home and not be seen.

Now, on the morning of Day Three of returning home to Canada from a Mexican vacation in lovely Puerto Vallarta (which had zero diagnosed cases of coronavirus and with no sports on T.V. or sports pools to distract me); it is time.

I actually began literally writing longhand on a notepad about three years ago while still in the hospital, recovering from what could have been a life-ending cardiac arrest. More on that later, but for now, what is most relevant is that I haven't been able to find the notebook I was given at the time. So a fresh start, with three years of added consideration of what to write about. Or probably more importantly what to leave unsaid.

You will note that I chose T.R. Shand as my pen name. My initials are T.R., for my given name of Thomas Richard, and I have been signing my name T.R. Shand ever since I began writing. My dad signed his name R.H. Shand, so I guess I just thought that's what you do. One year in elementary school, one of my teachers found it quite unusual that a seven or eight-year-old should sign his name that way and began calling me "T.R." My mom used to call me Tommy, and I was told that I was named not after the great Thomases (Aquinas, Jefferson, Edison et al) of the world but rather after her cat - yes, a Tomcat. As I grew older, I was more often called Tom but still am called "Tommy" from some relatives and sports buddies. However, I always thought T.R. Shand sounded like a good pen name and planned to use it as an author, including my first attempt at a book (about pirates for some unknown reason) in Grade Five.

My intention with "Tales to Tell My Daughters" is to entertain and enlighten, drawing from my experiences. In so doing, I have no intent to hurt or insult anybody. This will not be a tell-all or even a biography as, although biographies (Ali, Einstein, Napoleon, etc.) are high on my Goodreads list of books read, I have no pretension that my life needs to be captured in such a manner - by me or anyone else. So if you are mentioned, directly by name or inference, it is in good fun, and I hope you enjoy the read. Perhaps I even got your name right.

I recognize that my memory is not great at the best of times, let alone in reflections of more than 65 years gone by. So if your memories of various occasions differ from mine, I can accept that and look forward to hearing from you - hopefully not through my lawyer. I have not made an effort to clear my stories with any subjects involved but will leave out names if either I think that they would not be pleased to see them in print or, more likely, because I don't remember them.

Note to Reader: I am not a medical writer or expert, but I will provide some current COVID-19 (as it is now called) context to this story, as that is the world in which we live.

Just as common as procrastinating in starting such a project is not being able to end it. Often such tasks go on indefinitely. As a former newspaper writer, I work best to deadlines, so I am going to set mine as the end of my 14-day isolation period, March 31 (further note: Ultimately, I had more stories to tell beyond my self-imposed 14-day limit and so completed on time, then resumed).

In case, for some odd reason (or for Canada Health records), you want a record of this complete period, Day 1 was March 18, 2020, in which my wife Sheila and I opened our mail, read our newspapers, answered emails and phone messages, and had Wendy (one of my wife's eight siblings) buy us a few groceries. We also took our dog Coco for a walk and encountered one person we knew. We tried to maintain the recommended "social distance" of two metres, except for a closed fist, gloved greeting. Of all days to encounter Roger (our pickleball friend) on the street, after never having done so in years of us walking in front of his house, it had to be our first day of "isolation."

Included in the mail was a notice to have my now annual cardiac check and electrocardiogram in April. That is actually reassuring, not only relating to my heart as, although it seems to be doing well, I must admit that my levels of normal anxiety towards what can be expected in my "new normal" are somewhat heightened during this pandemic. I have experienced several bouts of pneumonia over the years, and that would not be a good thing right now.

Day 2: I made some notes for this project and contacted the bank, which has my dad's estate account. He died last October, a month short of his 95th birthday. I am the executor. I discovered that the person (Shamir) handling his account in Calgary was no longer with the company (CIBC). So, my email of February 28, including the order of probate, had not been received. A new person would be assigned but two weeks had been wasted.

We also discovered that our newly assigned financial adviser (Mathias) had left Scotia McLeod for greener grasses at Edward Jones. We would meet with him discreetly and at a distance, to discuss. He remembered our coffee order, so we will likely follow him, especially because we did not meet the new minimum thresholds for our previous adviser at Scotia McLeod anyhow.

Day 3: Let the work begin. I note that COVID-19 now has passed 200,000 diagnosed cases worldwide, with China calming down and Italy having passed China in terms of total death arisen. Alberta, where I reside, just recorded its first attributed fatality yesterday. I have had a bit of a cold for a while, but no other symptoms. We have not been tested. With our ages, my health history, and our recent return through airports, we are in a somewhat higher risk category than most, but tests are not being offered unless symptomatic - fever, dry cough, fatigue.

TALES TO TELL MY DAUGHTERS

Day 3: Do you like going to funerals? I do. Over the years, I have attended many; not just of loved ones but also to lend a measure of support to friends.

Actually, most times I do not go to the actual funeral although, with the many traditions, they too can be quite eye-opening. Most often, I go to a memorial service or what is usually referred to as a "Celebration of Life." I enjoy learning more about the deceased through the recollections of family and friends. I find both the reflections and their delivery to be very interesting - much like a biography, seen through the hearts, minds, and voices of those who cared.

This book is being written to capture some of those recollections of a life - mine - while I am still here (knock on wood) to share them. I don't have a desire to attend my own funeral, but I do like telling (and retelling) my stories - as did my father and his father before him.

I have two incredible daughters (Erin and Mackenzie), both young adults out on their own (in Jerusalem and Montreal, respectively). "Tales to Tell My Daughters" is for them, even if their reaction to contents may more often than not be "Oh, Dad. You didn't need to tell that story" or "Is that a true story?" Nevertheless, I hope they enjoy it. At least, I expect they will read it and share some comments with me, an opportunity which would not be there if these were only shared posthumously.

A Little Biographical Background to Begin...

I am now retired or perhaps semi-retired, depending on whether anybody still is willing to pay for my services (or whether or not I claim expenses this year with Canada Revenue Services). For several years, I have had my own home-based business, often while also employed. I have had several careers beginning in journalism, which evolved to not-for-profit, health-care-related public relations, and then into fund development, organizational management, and finally, into mental health advocacy. It has been an interesting ride to be sure and, like most lives, not a linear progression. As such, my home-based work could involve any of the above but almost always included communications and relationship building as integral elements and, I believe, as strengths.

I have been honoured to be chosen to emcee weddings and other events, both personal and work-related, and to even write obituaries and deliver eulogies. Some of my tales have been shared formally on such occasions but more often informally, and perhaps ad nauseum (for Sheila, and others most close to me). Hopefully, this book will be written in a manner such that you will enjoy the telling, even of those stories some of you have heard before.

I have been fortunate to meet many interesting people, some well known but most not so much, and have had a wealth of experiences. Most of my recollections told here will be first-hand, although some stories of family and friends are just too good to be left untold.

My story began with my birth, the first child of Richard (Dick) and Elizabeth (Libby) Shand in Montreal in November 1954. However, it will not be told in chronological order but mostly in themes or groupings relating to periods of my life.

I have to start somewhere, so I have chosen my time at Queen's University, 1973 - 77. In part, I so choose because it was a great experience, but more so as it featured some of the more colourful characters I ever met, as reflected in their nicknames - Grease, Bearshit, T-Bird, and Waffle

Thomas Richard Shand. Born Nov. 4, 1954.
Blonde and chunky baby.

CHAPTER ONE
LIFE BEFORE CHILDREN

Oil Thigh Na Banrighinn...

After having sung the chorus to the Queen's Golden Gaels fight song countless times, I must admit - I still have to Google how to spell it. My spelling is usually quite good, but this Gaelic phrase was beyond me, and the only word I actually got right was "Oil" - and that was a guess.

Queen's University is located in Kingston, Ontario, halfway between Toronto and Montreal. It was one of two universities to which I applied after high school (Royal York Collegiate Institute) in Toronto's west end. Queen's and Western are about equidistant from Toronto. They are both excellent schools, but I chose Queen's because it didn't have fraternities, which I do not hold in high regard. Little did I know that Queen's, despite having no fraternities or sororities, probably had more private school kids and old money per capita within its student body than any other university in the country.

I chose to register as a political science student, but after my first year, I changed my major to human geography and also finished with a minor in economics. I was trying to decide between journalism and law school as an ultimate career choice, but after spending about 40 hours a week between the radio station (CFRC) and the newspaper (Queen's Journal) during my four years there, I opted for journalism. Although Queen's did not have a journalism program, I had the opportunity to meet with the managing editor of the Toronto Star and my favourite columnist (Gary Lautens). They advised me to get my degree in what I wanted from somewhere that would allow me to practice journalism, as opposed to a school teaching it (which at the time were only Carleton U in Ottawa and Ryerson College in Toronto). They told me that wherever I went to work afterwards, it would teach me the fine points of journalism. For me, at that time, the advice was sound. Within a year or so, I was a sports editor of the newspaper and sports director of the radio station, doing play-by-play for Golden Gaels football and hockey while travelling all over Ontario and Quebec with the teams and my radio crew. It could not have been better or more enjoyable.

Me, circa fall 1973, at Queen's.

Almost all Queen's students came from away, and so lived in residence for a year. For me, that residence was fourth 'Leonard' - the top floor of an all-male residence. The top floor was fine, aside from when somebody 'papered' a room. One night, all the crumpled paper was taken from a papered room, thrown in the elevator, and sent to the basement. There it caught fire, burning out the basement cafeteria. The smoke rose and settled on the top floor, which not only forced us out (to the adjacent women's residence - oops) on a cold November night but also forced us to breathe in stale smoke for days following our return. Thankfully, there were no deaths, casualties, or long-term interruptions to studies - or to streaking, drinking (purple Jesus mixed and stored in ice in the bathtub), skating on Lake Ontario, or playing flag football on frozen fields.

But let's move on to Grease and the guys. They were my roommates for my final three years at Queen's, in an apartment off of Princess and Division, in downtown Kingston, about a half-mile from the main campus. One of the handier guys, Grease, drove a two by four into the ceiling of our three-bedroom apartment to create for himself a fourth bedroom, next to the balcony.

We did not know each other well but somehow came together and formed a wonderful living arrangement. I haven't kept in touch with them, but still treasure the three years we spent together. I hope this finds them well. As I seldom used their actual names back then, I won't share them with you now. But trust me, these are not fictional characters despite some of their stories sounding as if plucked from a T.V. sitcom.

'Grease' or 'Grik' was actually 'Tom,' but he proudly wore his nickname, come to honestly from his long, and often greasy-looking hair. He came from Bancroft, a small town in Ontario, wherein the summers he drove a "shit truck" for his dad, who had a septic tank business. Between summers, he studied geological engineering, and at one point was learning the violin while training to be heavyweight champion of the world - although he likely weighed no more than 160 pounds, soaking wet. He also used to warble a rendition of "I Have Confidence in Me," from the Sound of Music to psyche himself up for his exams. No, not your typical fellow.

As we had neighbours in floors below, it drove them crazy when they would hear Grease training, with a skipping rope, ala Ali. One day, Jo-Anne could stand it no longer and knocked on the door to see what was making the strange sounds. Grease was practicing his jabs at the time and caught her right on the nose. I am pretty sure it was the only contact ever made in his boxing career.

T-Bird was a math genius from Sudbury. I am not sure who gave him his nickname, but it derived from his last name, which began with a T. He was one of the top math students at Queen's, flying through graduate courses while still an undergrad. Among other things, he studied poetry - in Japanese.

Somewhere along the way, T-Bird met a nice girl named Brenda, who lived in a religious-type house on campus. On one of his early dates, he was attending a function there for which he baked cookies. Before the event, he strictly warned us not to eat any of these cookies, which he carefully wrapped and put in a tin to cool. I love fresh cookies, as did Bearshit, but we heeded his warning as he seemed quite serious about this - and the girl. However, Grease, who knew him best and longest, could not resist. He unwrapped all the cookies, re-wrapped his geological rock samples and put them neatly back in the tin. T-Bird did not discover this until presenting the cookies at the party. He was not amused, but I am still laughing at the prank almost 50 years later.

I too caused a good laugh at Brenda's expense. One afternoon, I was relaxing in the bath when I heard the apartment door open and the sound of Brenda and T-Bird coming in. I closed the curtain to the bathtub and stayed silent. I said not a word as Brenda entered the bathroom. It was not until she was well settled on the throne that I called out "G-day Brenda." I have never heard such a scream as she put an immediate halt to her proceedings and stormed out. I don't recall that she ever came back to the apartment. However, I think that she and T-Bird survived the many dubious experiences and hopefully can laugh about them now.

Queen's roomies (left to right): Bearshit, T-Bird, Grease and me (Mistah Shand)

Speaking of the washroom, with four guys sharing one, there was often a battle to get there first, especially in the morning. However, nobody could beat Waffle. He was maybe 5'4 but competed in trick skiing, had thighs like tree trunks, and could dunk a basketball. One day, we formed a human barricade in the hall to prevent him from accessing the bathroom. He just flipped over us, landing easily on both feet on the other side, and was the first to get in his morning whiz. Waffle was with us for just one year, but nobody ever came to match that trick.

"Bearshit" was also one of a kind and equally eclectic. Half French and half Irish, he was a high school all-star athlete from Pembroke, Ontario. His surname was Beriault, but he soon became Bearshit to us, pronounced with a nasal drawing out of the 'bear' sound. With a blue-collar upbringing, he came to us with a definite bias against people who came from wealth and privilege. He was determined to make good and become a medical doctor, and he eventually did, but not without some challenges.

He devoted himself to his studies, with no time for much else, including a girlfriend who moved to Kingston to be closer to him. One day, she phoned while he was eating from a tin. "Not now, can't you see I am eating my beans?" she was told. Needless to say, the relationship didn't last much longer than did the tin of Libby's.

In the summer of 1975, my dad took a job in Calgary and was on his own while my mom was left to sell the house back in Toronto. Bearshit and I came out west to keep him company. I got a job editing ads at the Calgary Herald, and Bearshit took on a job driving a milk truck for a family-owned business. On one of his first days on the road by himself, he flipped the truck and had a large jack come flying through the front windshield. He emerged unscathed, but the same could not be said of the truck. Nevertheless, he was not fired and ended up dating and marrying the boss's daughter. He set up a double date that summer, where I was to date the girl he liked, and he was with her friend. Don't ask me how, but everything seemed to work out for Bearshit; he survived the date, the driving job, and was accepted into medical school. I have since lost touch with him but heard years later that sadly, his wife died, and he has since remarried. It would be interesting if his kids have ever heard some of the stories of his earlier days. Bearshit, if you are reading this, we are long overdue.

We were actually all pretty harmless back in the day, as we all took school seriously and never did drugs or much drinking. However, we did seek the occasional distraction, be it hobbies, females, sports, or mischief. Probably, the most colourful was a bit of high-end end larceny of a downtown multinational - specifically, stealing the Gulf Oil flag from atop the flagpole at the Princess and Division gas station during the light of day at the city's business intersection.

Grease had the balcony view of the flag from his room and set out the plan for us. He would do the flag pole climb, while I created a diversion (exactly what, I can't recall) and the others posted watch from the balcony. I did my job and took off when I heard Grease yell, "got it." It was not until I returned to the apartment that I heard from the boys that Grease had caught the hitch on the flag pole on his slide down with the flag (you can guess what caught). It was several minutes later that he limped through the door. His prize was the dirtiest, greasiest, most useless piece of cloth you have ever seen - so disgusting that I am not even sure it made it home with him. However, the tale of the heist lives on and certainly was our greatest reward.

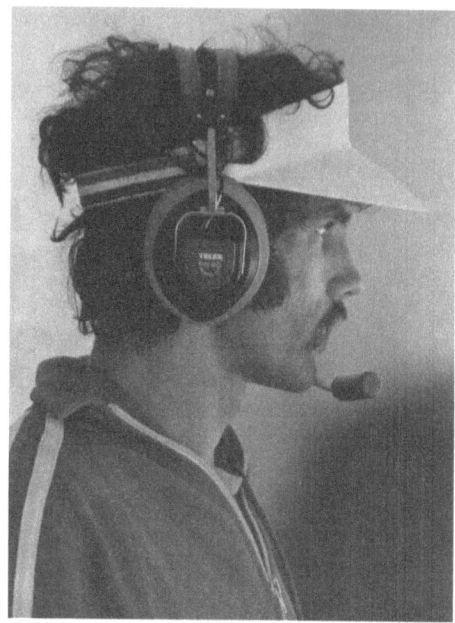

Sports broadcasting at CFRC.

By the way, if you are wondering what my nickname was, the most I ever got was Mistah Shand - obviously tame in comparison to those of my roommates. Hopefully, I was less boring than the nickname.

Day 4: The COVID-19 count in Alberta is now up to 195 diagnosed, one dead, and on the positive side; three now determined to be recovered. Sheila and I remain symptom-free except for my ongoing runny nose, which seems like I have had ever since my heart event. I woke up before 0500, not because of illness, but because I had so many story ideas. I am now thinking that this book will be done in two parts, perhaps separating my youth from my past 35 years with Sheila and our girls.

Today, I plan to continue with life at Queen's as there are just too many good stories to tell from that period.
As mentioned, I chose Queen's for a number of reasons, but was undecided about choosing to pursue a career in law or journalism. Needing at least three years before entering into a law program, I put my energies into working at the radio station and newspaper. It was one of the best decisions I ever made as I loved the work and met so many great people. In many ways, it paved the path for the rest of my working life, even though my career took a few twists and turns.

Tales to Tell My Daughters

First and foremost, the greatest part was the people I met, particularly those with whom I worked. At CFRC, it started with the station manager Steve Cutway, who was totally blind and totally amazing. One day, he invited me to bowl 10-pin with a blindfold. I think I only hit the pins three times in two of the 10 frames and scored a grand total of 17. It was hardly a good score but far better than our M.P. (and soon-to-be Liberal Cabinet Minister) Flora MacDonald, who not only missed the pins but threw her ball across not just one lane but two. Sadly, both Steve and Flora are no longer with us.

Also now passed is Peter Watts, who mentored me during my hockey and football play-by-play job. Peter had a great voice and was one of the first to join the new TSN network. He died in Calgary just a few years ago. After Queen's, I only spoke to him a few times, but hearing his voice on air always brought me comfort.

As it turned out, the person who succeeded me as the voice of Queen's sports was Chris Cuthbert, now one of the best sports broadcasters in Canada, still doing both hockey and football. I didn't know Chris at Queen's but know that he still holds Queen's colours dear. I sometimes wonder if that could have been me.

On my broadcast team were Jean Bangay and Rob Bruce. Rob was a local Kingston boy who primarily did the basketball play-by-play. I have not been in touch with Rob for years. The last time I heard from him was an invitation to return to Kingston for his wedding. I was working at the newspaper in Portage la Prairie, Manitoba (more on this later). I decided to go and booked my flight. Unfortunately, I did not notice that the wedding was actually 15 months away. I never did make the wedding or see Rob again, but I did have a lovely time revisiting Kingston and Queen's that summer.

Jean was from Toronto and still held on to her high school sweetheart from there. I was in touch recently when I saw a book, written for teens, by Jean Mills and reached her by email. She, Rob and I got along famously. If our paths were to cross again, I know we would rejoice in swapping stories and having a few laughs together.

One day, a photo of Jean and I public skating showed up in the Queen's Journal, unbeknownst to either of us. The pic was okay except for two small problems. We looked quite chummy, despite us never being a couple. More incriminating was that I was supposed to be in a Philosophy 101 lecture at the time the photo was taken.

I actually quite liked Philosophy - studying the works of people like Descartes and John Stuart Mills while exploring the basis of Logic. I did famously in my first term, but things took a dramatic turn later in the year when our prof, a man named 'Prado,' went off to a conference in the U.S. with a number of social workers. He came back totally depressed, thinking that his life's work had no meaning compared to the daily struggles of social workers. When he returned, my papers were suddenly deemed far too positive and euphoric in their outlook and were slashed to bits. I had no tolerance for his new outlook, so I continued to hand in my logic assignments and write the exams, but started going public skating instead of attending Prado's lectures.

Sometimes I have nightmares that I failed at Queen's, although my marks were largely good. Perhaps the cause was the two physical geography classes that I was required to take, one in soils and the other in climatology. Unfortunately, I was largely uninterested in them and thought it better to skip "the principles of" courses in the first term and go directly to the applied applications in the second term. I did not notice, nor did anybody tell me, that the principles were required courses to take the applied ones. Perhaps even worse was that both the prerequisite physical geography classes required completion of high school chemistry - a subject which I had also avoided. I managed to pass the courses due exclusively to the marks I acquired completing labs and the odd essay. But when it came exam time, I could barely understand the questions and was ready to walk out almost immediately. I left after the minimum 15 minutes and went to watch the Stanley Cup playoff game with the girls across the hall (as we had no T.V.).

The no TV issue came up again the next year - February 7, 1976, to be exact. That night Darryl Sittler scored 10 points against the Boston Bruins (arch-rivals of my beloved Montreal Canadiens). I had fundraised for our broadcast team to travel with the Gaels' hockey team to Sudbury but got waylaid by an emergency appendectomy, so I was in Kingston General Hospital recovering. On my very tight budget, I was too cheap to rent a T.V. for my room, thinking I could watch it in the lounge. However, I had no such luck and missed not only one of the greatest scoring feats of all-time, but more important to me, the humiliation of the Bruins. I never told my parents of this misadventure, but that is how it happened.

I found some of the political science profs more than I bargained for, and so switched majors in my second year to human geography - surprising even myself. Particularly off centre was a fellow named 'Perlin,' who tucked his pants into his high boots, ala Lenin, and taught, yes, Soviet politics.

Two other friends helped provide both friendship and broadcast training - Ted Kennedy and Shelagh Rogers. It seemed I was not the only person with a desire to work in the media who was advised to go to Queen's, as both CFRC and the Queen's Journal were filled with talented, aspiring journalists.

Ted was a thoughtful, quiet guy and the music director of CFRC. He had a great FM-style radio presence with a vast knowledge of rock. However, my best Ted-talk, as it were, actually came in the only class we took together: World Contemporary Economics, taught by Dr. J.J. Deutsch, principal of Queen's. He was not only principal but a leading advisor to Prime Minister Pierre Trudeau. This was the only class he taught.

The class was interesting enough, but on this particular day, the sun shone brightly through the window, causing both me and my buddy Ted to nod off. Dr. Deutsch saw us sleeping and got most indignant, raising his voice, saying "If you can't stay awake in my class, don't come." With this, I awoke, but Ted needed to be shaken. He was so embarrassed that he left and never returned to a single class.

Shelagh was classics director and ended up being a well-known CBC radio host. I don't listen to CBC radio, but we renewed our friendship years later when she ended up being a spokesperson and advocate for mental health, having survived her own depression. I see that she is currently Chancellor of the University of Victoria. Kudos to Shelagh. She is a wonderful lady whom I am proud to call a friend, and hopefully, one of the people who will give me feedback on this book.

Speaking of chancellors, the one at Queen's at the time of my graduation was Roland Michener, a former Governor-General of Canada. I only met him a few times, including the presentation of my certificate of graduation, but I was amazed that, with all the thousands of people he met, he remembered each by name, including me (my only other G.G. story was with the passing of George Vanier in 1967, when I heard a well-known broadcaster for CFRB Radio in Toronto announce: "Governor-General George Vanier died today. He was 78 degrees").

Like anywhere else, some of the Queen's profs were only interested in their research and publications, but most were fine, and, with my sports reporting, I only had a limited time to devote to my studies anyhow. Particularly challenging were weekends when the sports teams went on a road trip around the time when my papers were due. Being an arts student, a good portion of my studies were through papers, as opposed to exams. I was a good writer and so normally did well with the papers, and even enjoyed writing some of them, but inevitably there were not enough hours in the day, so I had to pull all-nighters.

I recall, after one of these, waking up on the couch with my whole body in spasm from exhaustion, and likely a lack of nutrition. That scared me a bit, so after third year I stayed back in Kingston for the summer, drove a cab at night, and took some courses to lighten my load in fourth year.

The Other Side of Kingston

The academic strategy played out well, but driving a taxi in the night in Kingston opened up a whole different world from what this middle class suburban white kid had ever seen.

By day, Kingston is a very conservative, staid old town, and Queen's students seldom venture further than a couple of the neighbouring pubs. Back in the mid-70s, it was also home to seven prisons within about 35 miles, including the only federal maximum-security women's pen in the whole country, as well as Millhaven and Kingston Pen - all delightful spots. Between the convicts sticking around after being released and their fascinating families and friends wanting to live close by, it made for a most interesting place to drive a cab, especially at night.

There were regular trips to liquor stores and houses of ill-repute, but I had two particularly memorable moments.

Once, near the start of my shift, I picked up two guys with a canoe. I put one in the back and one in the front; they held onto the canoe, leaning out the passenger-side windows. All was going well until a truck sideswiped me and took off - a hit and run. I quickly told the dispatcher who instructed me to "follow that truck" to get the license plate number. Still, with the guys holding on to the canoe, I put my foot to the pedal and, after a few blocks, managed to get close enough to relay the plate number. It was like a scene from a Chevy Chase movie, and I am sure the guys with the canoe got the ride of their lives. A while later, the dispatcher phoned to say that the police had caught the hit and run driver and recovered the truck he had stolen. No reward for me except a great story.

On another shift, later at night, I picked up two guys from a bar. They were beaten up pretty badly, and either had no money or were unwilling to part with it to pay their fare back home - perhaps four bucks. Glad to get them out of my cab, I told them to pay me next time, thinking/hoping that I would never see them again.

But, as luck would have it, I was called to pick them up about a week later at the place where I had dropped them off. Their cuts had healed somewhat, but this time they were carrying a motorcycle chain and a billy club with a thong. Surprise, surprise, they wanted to return to the bar where I had picked them up before.

So what did I do, stupid student driver, but remind them that they also owed me a fare from last time. After a bunch of colourful words were issued in a very threatening manner, one of them threw the money at me and slammed the door. Next, I heard a smash. I thought it would be my window or windshield, but the club was just hitting the metal pole beside the car. I said "thanks for the fare" and phoned my dispatcher to call the police to get to the pub asap. Not only did I have another great story, but also the fare paid in full.

I often chat with cab drivers now, and few seem to have had the colourful experiences that I had during my one summer of driving. However, in Kingston at the time, my experiences were far from the worst. One driver was forced at knife-point to drive to Florida, and another had his nose blown off and had not, but a pulpy mess left. I was lucky, as all I got were a few good stories.

My other favourite Queen's story culminated in a frozen field on campus, where I captained and quarterbacked the Fourth Leonard flag football team. We weren't a great team but had a few good players, and I was fast back then, with a good arm. It should have been safe as it was only flag football - no tackling. However, when you put a bunch of guys of mixed experience together in a competitive environment, anything can happen, and in this case, did.

John, my center, lived next door to me in residence. He was a good player and wanted to play fullback, but we needed his strength on the offensive line, which was pretty shaky. He also told me that he only had one kidney.

So we were in a shotgun formation, with me a few yards behind the line when he went to snap the ball but got kicked in the groin. The ball bounced back to me, and the defensive lineman who kicked him rushed in and picked it up. I was angry, and grabbed the guy by the shoulders and threw him down on the frozen field. His head snapped back, and he started convulsing. Minutes later, he was carried off on a stretcher and taken by ambulance to nearby Kingston General Hospital.

But the story doesn't end there. The other team went on to score, and I was on the return team for the ensuing kickoff. When the ball came to me, I was not clear-headed but decided to try and make the best play possible. I flipped the ball back to who I thought was my 'wannabe' fullback and went to become his lead blocker. The only problem is that I actually pitched it back to the ref who was wearing a very similar shirt to John. He stood there, mouth open, juggling the ball, then dropped it for the other team to recover. Needless to say, it was not my finest moment, but one I will never forget. As a footnote to the story, John actually dropped out of school in his second semester - he had a girlfriend back in Quebec and couldn't afford the long-distance bills. I am not sure what happened to the guy they took to the hospital.

That same winter, I got tired of lining up for food in the cafeteria, which was eventually re-opened, and decided to hitchhike down to New Brunswick during reading week (mid-February) to see my aging grandmother. She was quite possibly my favourite person and the sweetest lady I ever met (more later, see Chance Harbour). I convinced John's former roommate, Dave, to join me. We trained by fasting for days at a time, in case we should get stranded. The hitchhiking went well for the most part as people seemed willing to pick up two guys in all sorts of conditions - something most people would not do today. However, it was bitterly cold. After one ride, we got dropped on the other side of the bridge over the St. Lawrence River, leading into Quebec City. With it getting dark, we decided to start walking but did so hovering over masses of ice moving down the river, and across great piles of snow on what had been sidewalks. I spat and it froze in midair. I don't think that I have ever been so cold. We eventually reached our respective destinations in New Brunswick, and by the end of my visit, my great uncle George insisted on paying for my flight back to Kingston. It was perhaps not my most sane decision ever, but I never saw my grandma again, so it was worth it.

Having been exposed to some of Kingston's finest when I was driving a cab, in my last year, I volunteered to participate in a dance at the Federal Penitentiary for Women. I had always liked to dance but had never been in a prison, let alone dancing with murderers, drug addicts, etc. When I was told "back off, she's my girlfriend," I was quick to comply. Actually, most of the women I met were quite young and had come from tough backgrounds, involving drugs and abuse from men. I felt badly for them. One of them, with a huge gap between her teeth, was named B.J. I will leave it to you to figure out why. I actually ran into her in downtown Kingston later that year, but I don't think she remembered me. I enjoyed my prison time enough that I stepped forward to organize the next dance there. Again, not an experience that every kid from the suburbs gets to have or what my mentors at the Toronto Star meant when they suggested I go out and get some experience to write about. But if they are still with us, "thanks for the advice."

Portage

I was interviewed and accepted my first 'career job' over the phone from my friend

Tales to Tell My Daughters

Frank's kitchen on Inverleigh Drive in Toronto. Shortly thereafter, I packed up the 1966 Laurentian that I had bought for $200 that summer from my parents' neighbour, Mrs. Walker in Calgary, and I headed across the wintry prairies to Portage la Prairie, Manitoba.

It took a couple of days, and I slid off the highway a couple times en route. Somewhere near Wawa in northern Ontario, I stopped for the night and watched Warren Moon, on a little B/W T.V., lead the University of Washington Huskies to an upset win over Michigan in the Rose Bowl. Years later, I would meet him again in Edmonton as he starred for the Eskimos before heading south to the NFL.

Arriving in windswept Portage la Prairie and checking in at the Citizen daily newspaper, I soon figured out why they hired staff over the phone. It's far from being the most appealing spot in the country, especially in January. I was told that one aspiring reporter checked into the Portage Hotel, spent the night, and drove all the way back to Ontario without even staying for a day's work. It's windy, with terrible winters, so little wonder few people move there. Although, for a relatively small town, it's not the friendliest place for newcomers. I met some really decent people and, as has been the case most of my life, worked with some great people who quickly became friends. If nothing else, we were bonded with the shared excitement of starting jobs in the newspaper industry as well as complaints about life in Portage (as almost no one there calls it Portage la Prairie, the French heritage long forgotten). Everybody has to start somewhere, and, as well-educated cheap labour, they quickly threw us into the fire, in my case, literally.

Frank still tells the story of receiving a copy of my first bylined story in which my lead was, "there is never a good time for a fire." Later on, in the midst of the worst winter there in recorded history, my most dramatic story was also a fire as the Portage firefighters saved the town of Gladstone from losing its entire downtown in a massive blaze on the most bitter of days. My story was good, and the photos from our photographer, Sandy Black, were spectacular. With the fire, ice and danger, I have never witnessed anything like it. The untold part was that Sandy and I left town on our own initiative, as our news editor denied us approval to go to the story even though we had heard the firetrucks being summoned over our police band radio.

It was not unusual for the weather to be the lead story there for at least half the year. It was hard on both people and vehicles, especially $200 ones. One winter's day, I was out on a first date with Miss Portage Ex and had to hitchhike home 50 miles from Winnipeg as the car froze up and would not start. Neither she nor her waiting father was impressed, and the first date was definitely the last.

Another evening, also on a date of sorts, I was covering a member of the Winnipeg Blue Bombers (Bill Frank) speaking to a Christian women's group. To help me get through what I anticipated would be a pretty dry evening, I asked the publisher's assistant to join me. We got through the event fine until it came time to drive her home. She asked if I want to come in for a cup of tea, and I told her that I would park the car and be right in. The only problem is that the car decided that it would only go in reverse so, with no cell phones back then to call for help or inform her of my circumstance, I drove home the two or three miles in reverse, twice backing into snowbanks and needing to be pushed to get out. When I finally got to my own street, a neighbour was having a gathering, so cars were parked on both sides. With my back window very frosted, I somehow backed home through the cars, with inches to spare, and parked across from my basement apartment. An hour or so after leaving her parking lot, I phoned to explain. "You won't believe what happened..."

The car remained parked there, soon under several feet of snow, for the rest of the long winter. I decided to grow a beard and walk to work. I sold the battery for $25 and, in the spring, had the car towed, never to be seen again. However, that 66 Laurentian - my first car - served me well. It took me more than 25,000 miles, including from Calgary to Toronto and back to Manitoba. Not a bad return on a $200 investment. And the beard, a product of necessity for the bitter cold, was the best I ever grew.

I grew a beard in Portage to better deal with the bitter cold.

First Encounters

Portage was a lot of firsts for this boy from the suburbs: First job, first car, first winter on the Prairies, first exposure to the justice system, and first interactions with urban poverty, addictions, and homelessness, particularly as it relates to the Indigenous peoples. These firsts all came together in a couple of stories, separate but linked - at least to me.

Joe was a middle-aged Indigenous male who found various places to sleep at night in and around the main street of Portage, at least until it got too cold. Every winter, once it reached about 25 below, he would throw a brick through the liquor store window, sit down, and wait for the police to arrest him. One year, I was covering court when his case came up. The "*trial*" went like this:

"Ok, Joe I see you are back with us again," said the judge. "Do you have anything to say for yourself?"

Joe just looked blankly and shook his head, declining to comment.

The judge continued: "Well, it's late November now, it should be warmer by April. Is six months okay, Joe?"

Joe just nodded and was sent off to the Headingly correctional facility, outside Winnipeg, for six months.

Later that winter, I was working late and parked my car, the '66 Laurentian, near the newspaper office. It was very cold and I was anxious to get home. I came up to my car and saw movement inside. There was a young man, Indigenous and perhaps 17, under my dashboard on the driver's side.

I said to him, "What are you doing?"

He responded, "I am trying to steal your car. Are you going to call the police?"

I said, "No, just get out of the car, I want to go home." And he repeated, "Aren't you going to call the police?"

I repeated that I was not going to call the police and then told him that he would be better off to steal a more valuable car as this one was only worth $200 and would probably be considered only petty theft. Plus, it had very little gas in it if he wanted to drive it anywhere.

I have no idea if he had any relationship to Joe but it was sad to me that he was so young and already heading in exactly the same direction. And even sadder that both he and our society seemed to be accepting of his condition, and saw incarceration as the answer as opposed to seriously investing in treatment and measures to try and end the cycle of poverty, homelessness, and addiction.

Sadly, it is now 40 years later, and there may be more awareness and conversation about the issues, but they still remain, particularly in Western Canada.

In a reasonably short time, I became the lead reporter and was given the chance to cover the city hall beat and key stories such as the national election, where I met two prime ministers, Joe Clark and Pierre Trudeau. Although I don't recall their speeches, or what I wrote, both encounters proved memorable.

I caught up with Clark in nearby Neepawa, where he was making a campaign stop at the community hall to talk to local farmers. I arrived just in time to open the door for him and his wife, Maureen McTeer. Once inside, Clark was too nervous to even engage comfortably in conversation with small groups of locals, even though undoubtedly they were going to vote Conservative. McTeer was far more composed and appeared to have been better prepared to take on the PM role at that point in their lives. I met Clark twice after that in various roles, and I am pleased to say that he became far more comfortable with people and a fine statesman as he grew older.

I don't recall what Trudeau had to say that day, but I took a great photo of him in a classic contemplative pose. However, the paper was not willing to run it as he was a Liberal in a P.C. kinda town. That was the only time I ever met PET, but I subsequently did spend some time with his past wife, Margaret and son Justin, through mental health involvements. But more on that later.

I also got to know another political figure while in Portage. However, at the time, he was just a basketball player and a fastball pitcher. Brian Pallister was a towering 6'9 athlete, with a fiery temper. He was the centre of the Portage Beavers while I was their sixth man.

We played in the city league in Winnipeg and also in the Manitoba Winter Games, held that year in Dauphin. Our team held our own in league play, but the worst outing was one where I don't even remember our own game. It was the game before ours, and we were in the stands watching when a player went up for a layup, got pushed, lost his balance and went head-first into the concrete gym wall. We heard later that he never regained consciousness and died. The game meant nothing, but it was the first time I had seen a person die right in front of me.

T. Shand photo of Pierre Trudeau.

Brian had played for the University of Brandon and was certainly our star. He was even more intimidating as a fastball pitcher, leaping off the rubber and yelling as he released the ball, seemingly inches away from the batter. I think he has had to calm down a bit now as Premier of Manitoba.

I also played fastball but, with the rosters all set on most of the teams, I became the only 'white' player on the World of Tropic Stags, an otherwise all-native (nee Indigenous) team sponsored by a local pet store. I was a good player and fell one hit short of batting 400 - I think first or second in the league. I loved playing sports and was lucky, as a newcomer, to have the chance.

Our star player was a pitcher named Dennis Pashe, who was also a chief. He was a good pitcher but often got thrown out of games for throwing at players who rudely taunted him. Sadly, one of those teams was the RCMP, who would not be able to get away with such behaviour today.

One day I was out for a walk with the pitcher's brother, Steve. He remarked, "you know that my brother is a chief?" to which I said, "yes." "You know our last name, Pashe? You know what it means in our language?" I replied, "I have no idea." He proudly explained, "killer of yellow hair. Killer of Custer."

As we were in the neighbourhood of one of my friends from the Citizen. I suggested we stop by Bob's for a beer. So we sat down, and Bob popped open a couple of cold ones and proceeded to a large world map on the wall.

He pointed to the Bering Strait, separating Russia and Alaska, and informed Mr. Killer of Custer how the "Indians" of today came up from China, crossed the strait/land bridges and migrated down the west coast of North America.

Pashe just looked blankly at him. So Bob, clueless, repeated the story. Pashe then said, "are you calling me a f...in Chinaman?" Bob, now stunned, just said, "what?" Pashe repeated the same question. Bob, somewhat of a ginger, went red, looked fearful, and fell into immediate retreat but not recovery. He responded weakly, "no, that is just an old story that I heard. I am not even sure where I heard it."

I don't know what schools today teach to whom, but I am pretty sure that this bit of ancestral history was not captured in the curriculum for the Pashe family or likely anybody else on the World of Tropics Stags.

My other favourite story from my days in Portage involved the RCMP and the local dogcatcher.

I can't recall how I got to know Donnie, a local bylaw enforcement office/dog catcher, but he liked to tune me into happenings around town. One night he called and urged me to meet him for a police stakeout at a house in town. He told me that it looked like it could possibly be a good story.

Sure enough, shortly after I joined him, the SWAT team arrived from Winnipeg as there had been shots fired and people were being held at gunpoint inside the house. The stakeout went on well into the night until the gunman eventually surrendered.

In the meantime, Donnie told me about his life history and how his sister was his mother. All around, an interesting night.

But, for me, that was just the beginning as the next day I showed up at the RCMP office and asked for a report on what had happened the night before. The clerk there reported that nothing had occurred. I explained that I had been there, and while she could offer no comment, she was not allowed to lie to me. Nevertheless, she persisted in lying to me, saying nothing had happened.

It got even more interesting as my publisher, Ian MacKenzie, was also on City Council and Chair of Public Safety, including the RCMP. It seems that cover-ups were common in Portage, and such news was not expected to see the light of day. Only this time, they were caught cold and with a witness, my friend Donnie.

When I left Portage after two and a half years at the Citizen, one of the City Councilors said to me, "I can't say as I'm sorry to see you go. I think you set the town back five years." I responded, "that's fine, Jack, if I had not been here, it would likely have been 10." I am not sure how witty that sounds now, but I was quite pleased with that impromptu quip at the time.

Life also changed for me when Brian introduced me to a local girl from Langruth in a bar one evening. Phyllis was a lovely, kind person who would become a professor in Food Sciences. A few years later, she and I would return to Manitoba to be married. We would grow out of it after about five years and have not been in touch for many years. So, in fairness to all concerned, I will not go into any further details except to say that she is a good person, and I hope she is doing well.

One learns from every experience, and Portage was certainly no exception. But to say that I was eager to move on, both from a personal and career perspective, is an understatement. I was overjoyed to get the chance to head further west as a sports reporter for the Edmonton Sun.

Day 5: It is now Sunday and day five of our home isolation. COVID-19 continues to grow here as the number of diagnosed cases in Alberta is now 226. I am not sure whether I will write much today, but I did do some needed editing. I have set a target of 27,000 words (the length of the Hemingway classic 'The Old Man and The Sea') in 14 days, so I think I am about on target at 8600 words. However, the number changes as I go back to add and edit.

Sports and More Sports

Sports, playing and following, have always been a passion for me. However, although I had focused on sports reporting (newspaper and radio) at Queen's and had enjoyed every moment, it had never been my intent to necessarily stay in that vein professionally - I had done very little sports coverage in Portage.

However, to my surprise and delight, I was hired at the upstart Edmonton Sun, a member of the Toronto Sun chain, as a sports reporter. My first assignment was to meet with Eskimo General Manager Norm Kimball and to interview veteran quarterback Tom Wilkinson. I would meet Wilkie at a local racquetball club. I don't recall much of the resulting stories, but I do remember Kimball as being easy for a rookie reporter to approach and Wilkinson to be a great guy, who, despite his physique, was also a great quarterback. I doubt that he remembers that first assignment interview, but he still enjoys teasing me when I see him out with Eskimo alumni playing in charity golf tournaments.

Before too long, my lack of professional experience as a sports reporter caught up with me, and I was assigned to lesser profile beats, such as amateur sports and writing the sports section for the weekly T.V. guide. However, although the profile was lower, I discovered that there are even more great stories, and interesting people to tell them to, in amateur sports than in the pros, where answers are usually standard and rehearsed. Wheeling around the track with Paralympian star Ron Minor or getting insights from U of A's legendary hockey coach, Clare Drake, was more memorable than most subsequent interviews with NHL stars.

Covering amateur sports, I also was given the opportunity to get back behind the mic, including colour commentary for Doug Messier's St. Albert Saints of the Alberta Junior Hockey League. I got along okay with the grizzly senior Messier and met his teenage son Mark along the way. However, the G.M. of the club never thought my coverage had enough of a home bias, and I am quite sure that one night he had the bus leave Hobbema (now Maskwacis) without me on purpose when I was a little late getting my story phoned in (there was no Internet at the time). Fortunately, I had lots of experience hitchhiking in the cold, so eventually made it back to Edmonton without incident. And, as I couldn't prove intent, there were no ramifications to the Saints for leaving me behind. I am not sure what lesson was learned, but it probably was perceived as toughening up the "eastern wimp" - our new sports editor, Dwayne Erickson, was more than a bit of an old-school redneck. He ultimately died, essentially on the job, of long-term alcohol abuse - one of many old school journalists who suffered a similar fate.

A more pleasant assignment was being asked to interview Oilers' owner Peter Pocklington on watching the first home game of his Edmonton Trappers triple-A baseball team. To my surprise, Pocklington invited me to sit down between him and his wife Eva - for the whole game. Pocklington ended up leaving Edmonton as it's most hated citizen following the Gretzky trade to L.A., but I always remember him for the very kind way he treated a young reporter.

For the most part, I enjoyed working at the Sun but not so much the life around it. We were a morning paper, so we had a midnight deadline six days a week. With no Saturday paper at that time, reporters got a day off Friday and either Monday or Tuesday. That was fine for those who wanted to go out late-night drinking, as they were too pumped up to go to sleep after working to a peak late at night. However, I was more interested in playing sports or going to other events around town, which did not work with my work schedule. Ironically, by covering sports, I couldn't participate in them, especially team sports like fastball, hockey, basketball, and volleyball.

Ironically, it was not until after I left the Sun that I went to play fastball for the Sun team, coached by former major league slugger Wes Covington, who starred with Hank Aaron on the Milwaukee Braves in the late 50s. He was a very gentle man with huge, powerful hands. After having broken some metacarpal bones in my right hand making a diving catch, I ran into Coach in a local mall. He shook my hand, and I crumpled to the ground in pain. It was my final memory of a great guy who was not only a hand-breaker but a ground-breaker as one of the first black players to break the colour barrier in major league baseball.

I later moved on to slo-pitch and put together the Edmonton Sun Highballers, with some Sun staff and friends. From that, we built lifelong friendships, as strong today as they were back when we played. I remain in touch with many veterans of that team, including Brad, Barry, Smitty, Karen and Willy.

All Things Come to Pass

One day, after finding myself watching "Laverne and Shirley" in the late morning, and having seen the sorry state of many veteran sports reporters' personal lives at that time, I decided it was time to do something else with my life. As it happened, the choice was hurried along when I went to book holidays to attend the wedding of my friend, and first-year Queen's roomie, Alex Faseruk. Although I had provided plenty of notice, the Sun decided that they needed me during that period, even though I had covered numerous times while others were busy or away. I checked the law and found that they were within their rights to impose this upon me, so I quit my job.

However, my sports reporting was far from over as the person brought in to take my place, Con Griwkowsky, had been working on the side for United Press Canada/UPI. So when I returned from the wedding, I began covering the Oilers and Eskimos for UPC/UPI - something that I continued for about 12 years, including Grey Cups and five Stanley Cups.

There I got to regularly interview such Hall of Famers as Gretzky and Messier and did Goal magazine feature interviews with Paul Coffey and Grant Fuhr. I also wrote a feature on Jari Kurri that was featured on the front sports page of the New York Daily News. Fuhr spoke largely with very short answers but was still a good interview. I also always enjoyed speaking with Coffey, who tended to be more willing to actually express his opinions than most NHL-ers. The Kurri piece was also a bit of a coup largely as the talented Finnish winger was somewhat self-conscious of speaking in English. However, one on one, with plenty of time to formulate his answers, he was excellent. The resulting wire story marked the only time that my editors in NYC sent me a hard copy of a printed piece.

Leading the Oilers, of course, was coach Glen Sather. He had a well-earned reputation for manipulating the media to motivate his players. One day, during training camp, I saw him in the hall. He greeted me with, "Oh f...k, not you again? You never have anything positive to say." I took that as somewhat of a compliment and responded, "nice to see you again too, Glen. Had a good summer, did you?"

Surprisingly, the two Oilers I remember to be most well-spoken were Marty McSorley and Kevin McClelland, both brought in as tough guys but thoughtful in answering questions. Gretzky and Messier were strong leaders, and willing to speak with the media, but almost always were well-rehearsed in their statements. One time where that broke down a bit was at the press conference for the Gretzky trade. The "Great One" actually shed real tears, saying, "I told Mess I wouldn't do this."

UPC eventually closed operations, so interest in the CFL was lost, but not before I had the chance to cover such people as the aforementioned Warren Moon and Matt Dunigan. I enjoyed the work, the free food at the games, as well as the extra spends. I didn't get a lot of recognition as it was wire-service bylines, but I was told that I was ranked as the second-best NHL freelancer (next to the person in Pittsburgh). It probably didn't hurt that I got to cover Gretzky, and he, Mario Lemieux.

After leaving the Sun, I moved on to not-for-profit work, but my sports contacts remained of value as I later worked with Messier (Alberta Lung Association, Christmas

Seal Chair) and Dunigan (Canadian Diabetes Association, Dunigan Dash for Diabetes). I have always liked Matt, one of the most genuinely enthusiastic people you will ever meet. One afternoon, we were shooting a commercial that I had created to promote the Dunigan Dash for Diabetes. We were on the field of Commonwealth Stadium, along with a few teenage boys. When Matt asked me if I wanted to play catch, I could not refuse. I took off my dress shoes and ran a simple route, perhaps 10 or 12 yards deep. As soon as I made my cut-in, the ball was there, hitting me right between the eyes. I never even got my hands up to try and catch it. Matt immediately apologized, saying he forgot he was not throwing it to one of his teammates. I said, "that's okay. I didn't think that you had that strong of an arm." Not a bad line, but nevertheless, I was disappointed in the failure to make what should have been a simple catch.

Scoreboard at Commonwealth Stadium while filming a "Dunigan Dash for Dickville" commercial.

Sports remain of great importance to me to this day, although now it is more in the form of golf, pickleball, some tennis and ongoing sports pools (I love golf and considered including some stories here, but there are so many good ones that I have decided to leave them for another occasion).

Not being able to follow sports and sports pools is one of the real downsides for me of CV 19. My first pool was 1975 - 76 when Bryan Trottier, a rookie center for the New York Islanders, scored 95 points and led me to win the pool. I was pleased to be able to thank him in person for his contribution when covering an Islanders' Stanley Cup win here.

Day 6: A new week has started, and the number of COVID-19 cases continues to climb (259). The rate of new cases in Alberta seems to be slowing down, and, thankfully, the death toll remains at one. The isolation efforts, while certainly not helping the economy or one's social life, seem to be helping in slowing down the pandemic. Sheila and I remain symptom-free.

Passed My Peak Without Ever Reaching It

I have always loved sports and was once a pretty good athlete. I was the fastest boy in Junior High and was in the top one percent of male students tested for physical fitness in a Canada-wide centennial testing in 1967. I have never really enjoyed the rigors of training but loved to play, be it football, fastball, slo-pitch, tennis, squash, racquetball, pickleball, basketball, volleyball, golf, curling, hockey, or track and field. Although I have never been very flexible, I even did a little gymnastics, with some skills in vaulting and pommel horse. However, as much as I have enjoyed playing sports and had some success, I still feel some regrets that I never seriously pursued excellence in any of them at high levels. And what success and self-perceived skills I showed only add to that sense of lack of achievement that I describe as "I passed my peak without ever reaching it."

In looking back, I think that, like anybody else, I made my choices, which, in my case, have led to a balanced and good life. In this, I have remained largely true to my values but not necessarily committing to the sacrifices needed to strive for absolute excellence - whether that be in athletics, academics, or work. My choices may not have always been the best, but in looking back, I can understand why I made them. And most times would make the same choices if faced with the same circumstances. However, enough with the self-analysis and back to some stories...

Since I lived in Ontario, my high school was from Grades Nine through 13 - a big range when one was still very much in high-growth mode. I had experienced a great Grade Eight, probably the most fun of any grade, filled with good friendships and accomplishment, and the support and encouragement of my teacher, Mr. Anderson. After coming from Quebec, I took only about a week of Grade Six (and consequently still don't know much about the Aztecs, etc., that were covered that year). Then we moved from a townhouse in Mississauga to our house in Toronto. My mom convinced the school that I should be in Grade Seven - the first year of what would now be considered Junior High. I was fairly tall and very skinny with a blemished complexion, but I fit in quickly with new friends. I was quite happy to be one of the top students, both academically and athletically.

Can You Wiggle Your Toes?

When I started high school, I was just too thin to try out for football. Although not much heavier by Grade 10, I decided to give it a go. I was trying out for the flanker position, in what would now be classified as a slot-back. I could run and catch and appeared to have cracked the starting lineup when it all broke down, literally.

I was doing a drill when I was tackled, and my right cleat stuck in the ground. I felt an instant, very sharp pain shoot up my leg. I got helped to the sidelines, where I sat for the rest of the practice. The coach asked me if I could wiggle my toes and said I would be okay, and he would slot me in as the starting flanker.

The coach drove me home and helped me to the door of our house. He told my dad that I had hurt my ankle in practice but could wiggle my toes, so I would be fine. My dad, who loved football - and getting his meals on schedule - continued with his dinner and asked if I wanted to eat. From my position, lying on the living room couch, I said I wasn't hungry but that I was pretty sure my ankle was broken and needed a ride to the hospital. Dad asked if I could wiggle my toes then continued with dessert, which I also turned down.

After he finished eating, he said, "well, I guess I will take you to the hospital, just to have it checked out," and then proceeded to the car. After a few minutes, he came back in and asked if I was coming. I told him that I needed help to get to the car as I could not walk on my leg, and so he helped me out.

After examining my x-rays, the doctor came out and told my dad that I had broken my ankle in three places and that I would be admitted and scheduled for surgery the next day. Suddenly, my dad's outlook on my injury changed entirely: "Tommy's ankle is broken in three places. He needs surgery tomorrow, so I will need to be there," he told anybody who cared to listen. What was left unsaid is that his father (Frederick Barton Shand) was being remarried the day of my surgery. My dad had been most close to his mom, Clara, who had passed away, and he was not happy about his father remarrying, particularly to Gertrude, many years younger. My injury came just in time and was the closest I came to being a football hero.

I still have the pin in my ankle as a physical reminder of my mishap, but the story remains one of my most vivid memories. Two years later, I rejoined the team, only this time as a defensive back (corner). I went down again while making an interception, but this time the ankle was only sprained. I could still wiggle my toes, and this time there were no weddings or other tragic events to avoid.

T.R. Shand

Whenever one of my kids, or a niece, nephew or anybody else, with whom I feel compelled to share some of my life's learnings, should happen to compete for a championship, I urge them to treasure that time as it may not come their way again. It is actually a very common refrain even for those pro athletes who experience a championship early in a career - that they didn't realize how fortunate they were, and if they do so again, it is held even more dearly.

For me, one of my rare championships came at age 12 in peewee hockey. I played for a church hockey team coached by former NHL-er Hugh Bolton. We had good athletes, a star scorer, and, most of all, a coach who had us playing well as a team. I don't know if we were the most talented team, but we knew what it took to win. We often were local league champions, but this year, perhaps because of the country's centennial, we got to represent Toronto's Protestant churches in the city championship, played in Maple Leaf Gardens.

We were told that the ice surface was no bigger than those on which we had played all year. However, with perhaps only 100 spectators in an arena with seating for more than 16,000, the rink seemed enormous when we were on the ice. Despite the butterflies, we were ready and ended up being the only Protestant team to defeat the Catholics that day. The final score was five to two. I scored the third and winning goal, although hardly the first star as Kenny Winch had a hat-trick. In it's April 4, 1967 edition, the sports section of The Toronto Star described it as "he (Winch) counted an assist on Tom Shand's goal." So much for glory, but I did receive a quarter from my dad for scoring the winning goal, even though Winch was clearly the star. The Globe and Mail, covering the same tournament, got my name wrong but did have a photo of me, or at least my stick, which I could recognize as I had at least two different colours of tape on the blade (I can't remember why, perhaps I had just run out of black tape, but it did distinguish mine from others).

Over the years, our team attracted some pretty good hockey players, most of whom would never have set foot in the church (Royal York United) otherwise. As it was, they could be spotted in the pews with transistor radios and earplugs. It was also rumoured that some had removed more from the collection plate than they put in. I cannot attest to the verity of those reports, but neither could I deny the possibility.

Either way, it was great to be part of a winning team. And I can only remember one subsequent championship of any consequence when the team I formed, the Edmonton Sun Highballers, won the Alberta media slo-pitch tournament, held annually in

Red Deer's Great Chief Park over the Labour Day weekend. We competed every year and had a great time, but only once did we come home champions.

My Roots

I have mentioned my parents, Dick and Libby, a few times thus far but would be remiss in not further expanding on them and their influence on me.

Dad was the son of an engineer from Toronto (York). He had two older brothers (Jack and Ted) and a younger sister (Betty). He was predeceased by both brothers, but his sister, although recently widowed the same day my dad died, is still doing well. Dad's family grew up in Toronto and had a cottage on Sparrow Lake, about 100 miles north.

My mom was born in Winnipeg but grew up in New Brunswick, and every summer, we spent with her mom in the family home in Chance Harbour. It had been in the family since the early 1800s when our ancestors moved up from the eastern United States as United Empire Loyalists.

Dick and Libby met in Toronto, where my dad had graduated from the University of Toronto in Engineering Physics, and my mom was a senior secretary at the Toronto Star. She graduated from what would now be described as a diploma program from Mount Allison University in Sackville, NB.

Shortly after they married, they moved to Montreal, where they had me, and subsequently, my sister Janet and brother Jamie. As was the norm at the time, my mom stayed home and ran the household and my parents' social lives as well. They returned to Toronto in 1966, when the mailbox bombings in Quebec became too disturbing for many large Anglophone firms.

My mom and dad always seemed to be opposites, although they did combine to provide us with a sound and stable upbringing.

My mom loved Liberal Prime Minister Lester Pearson but hated his successor, the flamboyant Pierre Trudeau and never again voted Liberal after he came to power (I don't like using the word hate, but my mom was pretty passionate in her dislike for PET). My dad was less vocal in his political views but supported the Conservatives under John Diefenbaker then turned Liberal under Trudeau. They voted in every election but never for the same party.

Chance Harbour

Perhaps what had the most impact on me growing up was the choice of summer locations. Every year my mom took us with her to Chance Harbour, New Brunswick, where my beloved grandmother Mabel (Chadwick nee Thompson) and many of her brothers and sisters, spouses and offspring, lived on a point of land, edging out with rocky shores, into the Bay of Fundy and its frigid waters and world-famous tides.

My mom's dad, Ernest Chadwick, died when I was but a young boy. He had been gassed in the trenches in the Battle of Ypres in WWI. Brought up in Barrow-in-Furness, England, after the war, he returned to North America to help with recruitment. However, he never recovered fully from his injuries/illness and never talked about the war, not even with my mom. Our only source of information is the diary that he left behind. I don't remember him well, but I suspect I was most like him both in appearance and somewhat in character as he enjoyed listening to the World Series on the radio and, according to my mom, although he was often not involved directly in a conversation, he often contributed unsolicited comments from an adjacent room.

On the other hand, my mom's mom lived a long life, and I treasure the time I spent with her. As the oldest grandchild (in addition to our party of three, my mom's sister Janey had four children), I am pretty sure I was my grandma's favourite, and the feeling was mutual.

To this day, many of my favourite things (sound and smell of the sea, gingerbread, salmon, prunes, Scrabble, and The Sound of Music) are linked to my time with her and evoke fond memories to this day. Of these, The Sound of Music translates most to a story:
I was at a theatre, watching The Sound of Music with my grandma. When we sat down, she commented on the lovely, long dark hair of the girl sitting in front of us. Although I only knew my grandmother when she was older and her hair grey, I remember well seeing her take it out of a bun just before going to bed, and fully brushing it - long and lovely.

When the movie ended, she took a look at the woman's face as she exited. "Oh, what a pity," she whispered and then apologized endlessly to me. Nobody else had heard the remark, but it was the only time I can ever recall her saying anything whatsoever nasty.

Many years later, I took my brother (although only 14) into a bar in Calgary, where we saw the back of a girl with lovely, long dark hair. I thought she would be a good height for Jamie, so I asked her to dance. I was never as reserved or polite as my grandmother, but when she turned around, this girl had a face to stop a clock. My grandmother's words came back to me, although only shared later with my brother, who could not stop laughing at my choice.

Tommy and Grandma Chadwick in Chance Harbour.

Chance Harbour remains a special place for me, although more in memories of those who lived there than its actual current state as a little fishing village, where, as my favourite singer Stan Rogers would write, "most houses stand empty, old nets hung to dry, blown away lost and forgotten."

Chance Harbour is memories of:

- Watching Hogan's Heroes with my great uncle Charlie. One day he surprised everybody when he bought a bright red Barracuda. It looked lovely on his driveway until the day he forgot to put on the parking brake, and it rolled back into the Bay of Fundy.
- Seeing tourists from Boston and New England come up talking about "Yaz" and the Red Sox but going back with tall tales told to them by my great uncle Alf -

- with woolen plaid shirts and fishing boots hiked up over his knees.
- My great uncle George reciting his telephone number, which was multiples of seven, written out to about 100 places. And that same George, at 90 plus and legally blind, checking out my grandma's roof or walking across a crumbling breakwater to Crow Island.
- Chinese checkers and treats with my great aunt Grace and learning the names of every living creature in drives with my great uncle Ed. I was in their barn when lightning hit my grandmother's house and ran down the wire antenna for the old tube radio, setting the drapes on fire. My grandmother, alone in the house at the time, threw water on it and put out the fire. So much for not throwing the water on an electrical fire. What you don't know, or don't remember, won't hurt you - or something like that.
- Staying overnight at my great Aunt Polly's, to keep her from getting frightened by herself, and pouring down Coke floats.
- Singing songs around the piano at my grandma's with cousins Alice, Marilyn and their parents Charlotte and Jim, as well as cousin Eddie and cousin Murray's wife Clare, all of whom could sing much better than we could.
- Singing Danny Boy to my grandmother, who always encouraged me to sing when nobody else did. She also taught me La Marseillaise and the capitals of all 50 U.S. states.
- Climbing on an iceberg as a little boy, with the intent of riding it out to the Atlantic.
- Picking blueberries and playing softball with friends in the village, with fishing nets for backstops and lobster traps often left in the outfield. On my best day, I picked six bushels of blueberries and was paid the grand sum of $18. Back then, I could not close my eyes without seeing blueberries and can still conjure up the image.
- A year with a record 66 straight days of fog, sometimes so thick you could not see the end of the car when trying to drive and had to guess where balls were hit by the sound of the bat on the ball. It seemed like almost every year that we tried to fly to Saint John, we had to land in Fredericton and bus it due to fog. The one time that I remember landing in Saint John, as we walked down the steps from the plane to the tarmac, my mom told the stewardess (as they were then called), "jeez, Saint John smells worse than usual. Irving (who owned most refineries there) sure is stinking things up." The stewardess responded, "oh, that's not Mr. Irving ma'am, there's a boy throwing up on the steps behind you."... That boy was my brother Jamie.
- My grandma calling "Here gully, gully, gully," as she threw table scraps over the cliff to feed the seagulls.

- Hitting a crow with a rock as it was cawing from the top of a tree. To this day, the sound of a crow reminds me of my mom calling me "Tommmmmy."
- A few years ago, when my mom was still alive, Jamie and I (and our wives) bought one of my great aunt's houses, perhaps 500 yards down Crow Island Road, from where my mom had grown up. Chance Harbour was still pretty, but with only our memories left of our old relatives who made it home, it was just not the same place. There is something to be said about the sayings, "you can't go back there again" and "the people make the place." For many years, my only relative left living there all year was my cousin Stephen, a fisherman and also a really unique character. Sadly, he too has passed away. One day a few years ago, he cooked up lobster for Jamie, Frank, and me. That would have been great except for one detail. He neglected to tell us.

With relatives at Chance Harbour.

Sparrow Lake

Although we spent most of our summer days in Chance Harbour, we were fortunate to also have a cabin on a family estate at Sparrow Lake. My Uncle Jack and Aunt Betty had been spending all summers there since they were children and Canadian water ski pairs champions, with their dad driving the boat. Decades ago, my grandfather had purchased several acres of lakefront land about 100 miles north of Toronto. After my grandmother passed, there was a big fight about the property. Her will had never been set up properly, and the land, now of significant monetary value given its prime location in cottage country, was not even legally subdivided. Jack and Betty, who had been spending the most time there, persevered through the struggles and stayed on the property, while my dad and uncle Ted, the oldest, became just visitors. The property was beautiful, but it was tough to see the family torn apart in dealing with it. It was a story that I used as an example when, as a fund development person, I spoke to individuals about the importance of setting up their wills.

The Shand clan with grandparents Clara and Fred in the middle.

In addition to their water skiing, my uncle Jack also played major junior hockey for the Toronto Marlboros. I was told that perhaps he could have played in the NHL, but wages were so poor back then that he chose engineering. His sister Betty also skated professionally with one of Canada's great all-time figure skaters, Barbara Ann Scott.

My dad was a good athlete but a terrible skater and not a great water skier. He preferred football and canoeing, as well as tennis and badminton. He loved to tell the story of how he had saved a touchdown at Runnymede Collegiate when his nose clipped the heel of the opposing player. It was one of the tales I chose to retell in his eulogy last year.

However, the story I like best is one of a canoe trip he took with a buddy. Wanting to make sure he could cook a good breakfast over the campfire, dad insisted on taking his mom's cast-iron frying pan along with him, promising to not come back without it. Sure enough, the canoe tipped, and the heavy metal pan sunk to the bottom of the lake. Dad tried to swim down to retrieve it but could not go deep enough. So he climbed onto a cliff, dove deep, and after what seemed forever came up with the pan. It was a sad day when his mom passed as my dad said her death could have been avoided had she sought medical help for a heart condition. However, she had lost what would have been Ted's twin in hospital and never trusted doctors after that. Consequently, my dad was born in the kitchen. Knowing one's ancestry can come in handy, especially to know what conditions you may have inherited.

Interestingly, the Shand family members came together most often in recent years when one of us brought "Uncle Dick" back for an annual visit. Perhaps ultimately, by selling out his share of the cottage property for a relatively small amount, he maintained the affection of his siblings and his nieces and nephews. In all of our lives, there are consequences of every decision. In this case, we now sometimes wish Dad had left us some of the legacy of the lakefront property, but we are delighted to be so well received (by cousin Donna et al.) when we go back for a visit.

My family at Sparrow Lake. Left to right: Me, PopPops, Erin, Mackenzie and Sheila.

Oddly, some of the best stories of Sparrow Lake were after Grandma Shand had passed, and Gertrude joined the family. She had met my grandfather in Florida but also owned a property in Bala, a little further north in cottage country. She was a busty lady, which was amplified when she used to carry around her Chihuahua in her cleavage. This was all the more repulsive to us as my grandfather had always owned beautiful, full-sized collies and used to shoot chipmunks, which were far more attractive than the little rat-like thing that Gertrude carried around with her.

I think my grandfather remarrying bothered my dad most. This was most evident one day at the cottage when he asked if anybody had seen his dad. Jamie innocently piped up, "I think he went necking with Gertrude in the boat." Coming from this tiny little guy, we thought this was hilarious, but my dad pretty much gagged on the spot.

In short, I have been lucky and proud to have come from such strong and supporting families - particularly the Shands and Thompsons who most strongly influenced my growth as a person; and we remain close. I feel equally proud of the heritage left to my daughters from my wife's family, the Littlefairs (more later.)

Day 7: Now, halfway through our home isolation, we remain okay, although the number of diagnosed cases of COVID-19 in Alberta has risen to 301. Governments continue to take measures, but the biggest story so far today was the announcement of the cancellation of both the Memorial Cup junior hockey championship and the Tokyo Olympics. Both will be huge disappointments to the athletes and all those involved in hosting, but it seems there was little choice but to cancel.

Here at home, I woke up at 0200 and, with a number of stories going through my head, I didn't get back to sleep for a couple of hours. I will need to catch up on the missed sleep but am happy to have taken on this task.

Me at a high school science camp in Toronto.

High School - Not So Confidential

Many of the thoughts which came flooding back to me were from my high school days and the teachers and friends who made it interesting. I will list some of the more memorable moments. In no particular order, I recall:

- Mr. Scanlan, my Latin teacher, walking back and forth in the classroom, carrying a Roman axe prop and talking to himself in Latin. I never knew whether, in his mind, he actually thought he was speaking to Cicero and Caesar. Either way, it made a rather dry subject more entertaining.
- History teacher Ms. Harding repeatedly emphasizing that we must remember that the Battle of Hastings was in 1066. I can't say as I remember quite the full significance of that event. Still, if the question ever comes up in Jeopardy, at least I have not forgotten the date.
- Math teacher Mr. Matlock telling the whole class that my notes looked like a "dog's breakfast" and the philosophical statement that "what you gain in the bananas, you lose in the peaches" - or maybe it was the other way around.
- Sharing a 26er of Canadian Club whiskey with friends over a lunch hour. That afternoon, I suddenly started answering math questions, but nobody seemed to notice when I fell asleep at my desk in creative writing. At least, I didn't fall down running around the track like one of the guys.
- I didn't have much use for Grade 13, which was only being taught in Ontario. I had already been accepted into Queen's, based on my Grade 12 marks, so I left school early to start a summer job (acting manager on summer relief for National Trust branches across Toronto). I also often skipped classes to play bridge with my buddies. I still did fine, but my mom was embarrassed at my graduation ceremony that I had not scored better marks during my final year.
- Attending my first paid concert with my friend Dave Cunningham. We saw Liza Minnelli, fresh off her huge success with Cabaret, at Massey Hall. In retrospect, one may have wondered if we were straight, but the thought never entered our minds. I also ended up going to a couple of great free concerts with friends - Lighthouse, in the pouring rain at Nathan Phillip's Square in downtown Toronto, and Chuck Mangeone outdoors at Ontario Place. They were totally different styles of music, but I enjoyed each thoroughly.
- After having danced to "Me and Mrs. Jones" at a friend's party, I went out with a girl a couple of times then asked her to be my date to the Grade 13 prom. She was only in Grade 12 and had a purple Duster and a shag haircut, like Jane Fonda in Klute. She told me "nothing personal" but that she was "waiting to be asked by somebody special." Neither of us ended up going that year. I don't remember her name, and I'm quite sure that she long ago forgot mine.

- An even more story-worthy tale came to pass with a girl I knew, from a pair of identical twins. I don't remember which one but they were both nice, and I thought just friends. We were with a group of friends on an overnight camping trip. We cooked Gin and Wink in a pot over a campfire, breathed in the fumes and drank it hot. Apparently, I had too much as, a week or so later, I had no idea of what I had done to be pulled off into the linen closet of the Abbey Road Pub in Toronto where the young lady said she wanted to marry me. I politely declined the offer, but It was not until about 40 years later (at a triple-wide in Palm Desert, with my friend Orrin) that I took my next drink of gin.
- Royal York still stands but several years ago became the Etobicoke School of the Arts. But like Queen's or Chance Harbour, it is not the setting that I remember without the friends I made, many of whom (e.g. Frank, John, Alex, Wolly, Rob, and Brent) remain my friends some 50 years later, despite us not living in the same part of the country.

Moving from Montreal

As mentioned before, our family moved from Montreal to Toronto (with a brief stop in what is now Mississauga before we settled at 14 Adelpha Drive), a walking distance from the subway stop at Islington and Bloor. For many years, my dad worked downtown and walked back and forth to the subway, which was good for both his physical and mental health. When his office moved to the other end of the city, it was not so pleasant as he hated the daily drive on the 401 (my uncle Dave, whose office moved from the east end to the far west of the city once commented that some days he would have been quicker to catch a plane to Edmonton than drive home to Markham).

I enjoy going back to Toronto, seeing friends and exploring parts of the city I never knew. However, despite the urging of my friends there, I never had a desire to move back to Toronto or, for that matter, to Montreal either. The large mega-cities are great to visit, but the traffic and costs of living are too high for my taste. Edmonton is about the limit for me, and somewhere smaller would probably be better still, now that we are retired.

Although I was leaving behind friends and having to put up with coverage of Toronto sports teams (then just the Leafs and Argos), I actually didn't mind moving from Montreal to Toronto. In the thinking of an 11-year old, the weather would be warmer in southern Ontario, and we would get many more English T.V. channels.

I would miss the snowball fights on the way to school and the resulting trips to visit with the vice principal. I had a live arm and enjoyed throwing things. One day, I was firing snowballs at front doors on the way home, when a lady a couple of blocks away opened her door, and my snowball went right into her baby carriage. My mom somehow heard about this before I even got home and was not impressed.

Getting together with high school buddies John (left) and Frank (right).

Although my mom was at home all day, somehow, way before the invention of social media, she seemed to get word of what was going on. To this day, I don't know how she got hold of a letter I sent to a girl in Grade One, proposing to her and offering to buy her a diamond ring and take her to Africa with me to train the animals. The only thing I remember about Janice was that she was the smartest girl in Grade One, and her response was a simply stated, "drop dead."

The other day I clearly remember from my youth in Montreal was November 22, 1963. I was asked to take the class attendance records to the school office and heard that JFK had been shot in Dallas. When I got home, I can never remember my mom being so upset.

For whatever reasons, perhaps because so much of our news comes from the U.S., I have had a great interest in happenings there. One of my most treasured possessions is a bust of Abraham Lincoln, which was given to me by a great Aunt, who herself lived to be 100 - and I think the bust is even older. I also have a library full of books on JFK and his brother Robert, who I saw one summer in Toronto at an Argo game at CNE stadium. I also remember where I was when I heard about the deaths of:

- Elvis (when I was on the roof, painting a house, followed by a horrific afternoon in a dentist chair, listening to Elvis music while my mom's dentist tortured me);
- Martin Luther King (while I was watching an NHL playoff game on T.V.);
- John Lennon (While I was working at my desk at the Edmonton Sun); and
- Stan Rogers (smoke inhalation from a plane crash in Kentucky) in 1983, while I was working at the Alberta Lung Association.

I have always been an avid fan of the arts (music, theatre, literature, movies and painting). Although not personally gifted in any of those pursuits, I do support and follow them, and have tried my hand at most. I enjoy being on stage but have been limited, by my lack of talent, to playing clarinet in our high school orchestra, and minor acting parts in stage productions. Perhaps the only place where I have had a modicum of success in the arts or onstage is in being an emcee for various events.

However, over the years, I have attended innumerable theatre plays, concerts, and festivals, as well as ballet and other dance performances, amateur and professional, big and small.

One of my most memorable moments came during my first trip to New York City, where I found myself alone (except for a security guard at the door) in the Museum of Modern Art with my favourite painting, Van's Gogh's The Starry Night. I have been fortunate to have many other special moments, such as:

- Les Miserables, for the first time, on Broadway); and
- Michael Buble with David Foster (in a room with perhaps only 10 tables of people in Prince George) being two that come to mind but, aside from dance performances from my daughters, nothing has ever taken my breath away as my time alone with that painting.

CHAPTER TWO
MARRIED WITH CHILDREN

Day 8: Sheila and I are now in our second week of home isolation from CV-19. The number of diagnosed cases in Alberta is increasing (now 359), and an elderly person in a multi-care facility in Calgary has died. Isolation and social distancing are undoubtedly helping slow the spread, but most people expect the worst is yet to hit us, and numbers would certainly increase more if more people were being tested.

In terms of this project, I finished the first part, which is basically limited to the first 30 years of my life. Although I would be okay with leaving things there for the time being and seeing if there is any interest in reading this material, I did commit to writing more. And there are lots of tales still to tell, so I will continue with Chapter Two, and see where it goes.

The Big Bang

I will start Chapter Two with what I will call 'The Big Bang.' Early on the morning of February 26, 2017, I collapsed on the bathroom floor, fully unconscious. It caused a big bang that Sheila heard downstairs. I am retelling this story from her reports as I don't remember any of what happened at that time or most of that day. The next thing that I recall was several days later waking up to my sister-in-law Ruth and her husband, Ken. I was in an ICU bed at the Mazankowski Heart Institute in Edmonton but assumed I was in Calgary as that is where they lived.

My next memory was singing "Old Man River," which I often do when my throat is scratchy, just to see how low I can go. My brother Jamie, also from Calgary, caught this on tape, although I don't watch it as I prefer not to relive those times.

I subsequently learned that Sheila, who had woken up with me in the early morning when I said I wasn't feeling well, went down to the family room. Oddly, she saw a TV.

commercial about taking blue daily aspirins as a precaution to prevent heart attacks. I did not have a pain in my chest or other symptoms but did go upstairs to take a blue aspirin or two. Apparently, the paramedics found them in my mouth as they tried to revive me.

I now make an annual trip to our local fire station on February 26 to thank the firefighters for their efforts in saving my life. But cardiac doctors have told me that the person to whom I owe the most is Sheila, who not only came to my rescue but also performed CPR on the spot, even breaking my ribs as one is supposed to do. Fortunately, she recalled her Red Cross training from years before and did not hesitate, with her determination overcoming her fears.

Since then, we have both learned what is meant by my "new normal." It is getting better but likely not with the same level of energy and physical strength as I had prior to my heart "event" (I have been responsible for running events most of my adult life, and although I would not choose that word to describe what I went through, it certainly was a life changer, medically, physically, and psychologically).

While I have no desire to relive the experience, people are very curious, and I don't mind sharing some thoughts. Firstly, of course, I encourage people to take better care of themselves. And, if at an age where their risks are higher, to get themselves tested, as my attack came without warning even though I had 100% blockage of my main artery.

Secondly, although I technically was brought back from the dead, I have no recollection of that time - no lights, voices, or other unconscious memories. It's too bad, in a way, as it would have made for a possible bestseller.

After losing about 30 pounds, my weight has leveled off between 175 and 179 pounds. I can no longer run any length or speed and have also slowed down my golf swing. However, I did meet my goal of playing golf before the end of the season; albeit, with a cart. I am now starting to get some distance back and have walked an executive length course. I like walking the course, so I hope to walk 18 holes now and again this summer.

What was most surprising to me, although not to my cardiac team, is that it was just not physical exertion that fatigues me, but also social interaction. After an extended day of activity, it would take me about a day, usually on the couch, to recover enough energy to do normal daily activities.

I am pleased that this has gradually improved, but I was worse than I realized when I went back to work only about three months after the event. Hence, in large part, my premature retirement, prior to age 65, which was my intent.

Other measuring stick activities for me were walking in the five-kilometre New Year's Day YMCA walk, which comes by our house every year. I was one of the slowest out there, but Sheila and I finished it despite being bundled up to survive the -25 C. I also completed the hike up the huge hill at Masada in Israel in exactly opposite conditions - blistering heat. It took me about 150 minutes, about 30 minutes behind Sheila and some others in our party. Mackenzie, always worried about her dad, stayed with me, as did Jamie, who probably also benefited from the rests and slower pace. By the end, I was exhausted but literally bought the "I climbed Masada" t-shirt to commemorate the occasion.

It is impossible to forget my (main) event, but, as time goes by, my new normal is slowly evolving, and I am fortunate and grateful to be here to tell the story.

Surprise Wedding

It is probably as good a time as any to more formally introduce my wife Sheila - the heroine from the previous story.

It is not unusual for the two of us to be caught watching "Say Yes to the Dress," from either New York, Atlanta, or Toronto. Besides filling some time while we are drinking weekend coffees, the people and their circumstances portrayed are often interesting. However, perhaps more curious is that Sheila did not experience any of these situations with our own wedding. In fact, she did not even know about the wedding until the day before when the Justice of the Peace needed her mother's maiden name to complete a form.

Sheila had time to get her hair done but little else, and when I came home from work, she asked, "Is there anything you want to tell me? A Justice of the Peace called today and asked for my mom's maiden name."

I responded, "stupid man, I told him it was a surprise." I had told Sheila that we would go out to dinner with her sister Wendy and her dad (and their respective partners) to celebrate her birthday, which was the next day.

However, I had arranged not only for dinner but also for the JP, Wendy, and Steve as maid of honour and best man, respectively (although I had to tell Wendy the truth

55

since she and Steve were not feeling well), the music (Whitney Houston on video singing Greatest Love of All), and for our friend Willy to take photos. And, oh yes, I had also picked out Sheila's dress for the occasion.

Our wedding dance to Whitney Houston's "Greatest Love of All."

We had both been married once before, co-owned a heritage house in Edmonton's Old Strathcona area, and had a daughter - Erin, who months earlier had presented an engagement ring to Sheila (hidden in a tin of tennis balls). So being married was not really new to us, but the timing and details of the wedding were a total surprise to Sheila, the bride.

As it turned out, there were also a couple of surprises on the wedding day. Firstly, it had rained that morning, and our patio furniture was still wet. It was not until Willy took photos of the wedding ceremony in our living room that we noticed that the back of the Justice of the Peace's clothes were very wet. I also didn't turn off the video machine after hearing Whitney's song and found out I had taped it over an Expos baseball game - as I recall a no-hitter by Dennis Martinez - which came on before the end of the ceremony.

Unlike some of the temperamental brides on TV, Sheila took it all in stride, saying, "I should have known you would find a way to sneak in the Expos somehow."

The Other Loves Of My Life

Speaking of les Expos, what a perfect segue to one of the other loves of my life - my pro sports teams - and pools. Having all sports postponed because of coronavirus has cut me off from one of my favourite passions - following my teams and pro sports pools. I miss them as, for years, I have missed my Expos. Cheering for Washington, where they relocated, is just not the same, even though they won the World Series last year as the Nationals.

There are now rumours that the Expos could return to Montreal in the future, but for now, all I am left are memories, some great (of players like Andrew Dawson, Andres Galarraga, Coco Laboy, and John Boccabella, to name a few of my favourites) and some of losing more than 100 games in a season. It's a wonder that I came out of adolescence relatively unscathed, as I was saddened by every loss.

So too have I suffered through my Minnesota Vikings being the only team (aside from the Buffalo Bills) to lose four Super Bowls and never win one. I have been a Vikings fan since 1967 when Bud Grant moved from Winnipeg in the CFL to coach the Vikings. Cheering for the Vikings has not been without great joy and anticipation of upcoming games. Perhaps most prominent were the days of Alan Page and Carl Eller - the Hall of Fame defensive linemen who led the Purple People Eaters. They were fierce and played home games in an outdoor stadium, where Grant did not allow heaters for his team, even during the most frigid days. Other personal favourites include quarterbacks Fran Tarkenton and Warren Moon, as well as running backs Chuck Foreman and Adrian Peterson; and of the current players, hard-hitting safety Harrison Smith. The latter reminds me of my all-time favourite D.B.: Jack Tatum, for whom I chose to wear the number 31.

North of the border, I am also a long-time fan of the Montreal Alouettes. Times have not always been good there, on the field or off, but I am loyal, and my hopes for more Grey Cups remain high. Oddly enough, when we lived in Montreal, I cheered for the Als, but my favourite players were Bernie Faloney and Hal Patterson of Hamilton and receiver Whit Tucker of Ottawa. I had many favourites on the Als over the years, but foremost was receiver Ben Cahoon, a fearless target in the clutch for, most notably, quarterback Anthony Calvillo.

With respect to the NHL, I was born in Montreal, so never have I strayed from my love for Les Canadiens, starting with the Rocket and Jean Beliveau right up to current days with Carey Price and Brendan Gallagher. Not only have they won more Stanley Cups than any other team, but they have done so with class and style - a tradition that is widely recognized, particularly in how they honour past players.

I once held Toronto Argonaut season tickets and covered many seasons of Edmonton Oilers hockey games, but I have remained loyal to my Montreal teams, as well as the Vikings. I remain optimistic that this virus will soon be behind us, and I can get back to my sports - even though the Canadiens appear destined to miss the playoffs again if playoffs are even held this year. (Ed. note: NHL playoffs were held and Canadiens beat Penguins in first round.)

Introducing Two Amazing Girls

People often refer to occasions as being the happiest in their lives, aside from the births of their children. Not to take anything away from the miracle of bringing a new life into the world, but I feel that my pride and joy for my children has only increased with each passing year. I could not feel more proud of who they have grown up to be. However, let's look back at day one for each as both were quite remarkable.

At Niagara Falls- Me, Erin, Mackenzie and Sheila.

Erin was born on Boxing Day as Sheila lost her appetite for Christmas turkey and went into a long labour that eventually ended with a C-section. As such, her sister Ann and my sister Janet both held Erin before Sheila.

The funny part, although, at the time, not so funny to Sheila, was that her doctor was not around since it was Boxing Day. However, with the Misericordia being a teaching hospital, there were plenty of students in on rounds. After a few visits, it became obvious that a recent class must have emphasized that the pelvic opening had a relationship to the size of one's feet. After the umpteenth student had asked Sheila for her shoe size, she finally had enough and said, "is there a god-damned shoe sale at West Edmonton Mall or what?"

Despite her mother's stress (and small feet), Erin emerged absolutely beautiful even if I do say so myself.

Four years later, it was Mackenzie's turn to join us. She, too, arrived by C-section, only this time, the doctors did not put Sheila through as much stress before going in that direction. The other huge difference, for me, was that because it was planned, I was allowed in the operating room to not only witness the birth but to cut the umbilical cord. It was like an out-of-body, totally surreal experience to first see Sheila from the inside, and then to help remove our child from within. I have never experienced anything so remarkable before or since. And she too was beautiful - at least until she caught Erin's pink eye.

From time to time, my girls ask me whether I miss not having had a boy. I can say quite honestly and wholeheartedly that I would not trade my girls for a boy - or anyone. I am so proud of both of them, and they have brought us such joy. However, that is not to say that I wouldn't be delighted to have a grandson sometime in my future. No pressure - and a granddaughter would be perfect as well.

Dance Dad

Both girls danced from an early age and continued for many years. Erin was the stronger dancer of the two and became a professional contemporary dancer (Toronto, New York, Israel). However, my greatest pride came not from their medals or acclaim but for the life lessons they learned through the process - discipline, hard work, artistic expression, athleticism, teamwork, and learning how to accept winning and losing.

For Erin, this notion was best reflected when, at the Prince Rupert Dance Festival, she forgot a big part of the newly revised choreography for one of her solos. We were not familiar with the steps but noticed something was off. However, she completed the dance and afterwards came up to us. She did not utter a single excuse or complaint (of changing the choreography at the last minute or having to remember too many dances.) She told me, "Dad, I forgot my steps. It will never happen again." I said to Sheila, "I have never been so proud. All the money and time we have spent on dance lessons have paid off."

Mackenzie grew quickly when she was young. She never forgot her steps but was not quite as adept as her sister in executing them. One day at a competition in Burns Lake, she brought tears of joy to my eyes in beautifully performing "Send in the Clowns" but had the misfortune of tripping on a staging curtain as she exited. I looked past the mishap and thought she had done great, but the judges picked her fourth of four competitors. She was upset with having let her studio down, and I was upset with the judges for not at least tying her for third. But we had a great talk afterwards to remind her that she was not dancing to win but for the joy - and I was proud of her, regardless of how she finished.

Odyssey Dance, with several parents.

Years later, after having the courage to try out for the prize-winning cheerleading team at her new high school (Harry Ainlay) in Edmonton, Mackenzie was eventually cut from the team as she didn't have the arm strength to hold up others in the pyramids. Instead of getting upset, she set up a workout program to strengthen her upper body. To this day, her strength and fitness are outstanding.

Both girls are also tremendous friends for others. I never recall friends of mine supporting each other's emotional needs as we grew up. I don't know whether it is a difference between boys and girls or a sign of changing times. Either way, I am tremendously proud that they are such caring individuals - even though their caring for their dad post-heart events sometimes reaches epic proportions.

Our girls live a long way away from us (Jerusalem and Montreal), but in many ways, they are as close to us as ever, often connecting by phone or social media, or delighting in joining us on holidays.

Day 9: The number of COVID-19 diagnosed cases in Alberta continues to rise, now 419, with 61 new cases. However, we have not had the exponential increases seen in some other countries, so hopefully, the restrictions imposed upon people here (including us) will somewhat limit the spread.

In the meantime, now that completion of this book is just a few days away, this morning, I sent out a teaser on Instagram with regard to its (limited) release online.

Holidays Cherished

Annual Family Christmas Card, 1991.

Sheila and I share quite a few common interests, such as live theatre, music, television, family, and a shared desire to go away on holidays. Now that we are retired, we have more time to do so, but even when working, I can't recall a holiday spent at home. We have always used our vacation days, plus as many as we could borrow, to experience life elsewhere.

Vacations have included escapes to various winter vacations, including Arizona, California, Hawaii, Florida, Panama, the Caribbean, and Mexico. Winter is simply too long and cold in Canada. This year, we also experimented with spending almost all of November on Vancouver Island. We had enjoyed times there before but always in the summer. This time, we wanted to see what life was life there without the horde of tourists and in less ideal climatic conditions. We also toy with possibly moving there someday - if and when housing market prices allow (we actually listed our house in Edmonton last summer, but the market was absolutely dead and there was almost no interest).

We have also been back and forth across Canada, and over the border to New York City and Chicago, last summer. It was our third attempt to get there. Previously, we had intended to go to a conference there on September 12, 2001 - a day after 9/11. That was obviously a no-go. We tried again a couple of years ago, booking a United flight overseas from Chicago, but our luggage was delayed en route in Montreal, and we never had time to make it any further than O'Hare airport. Fortunately, the architectural river cruise which we had booked was refunded. We tried again last summer on the way back from Portugal (again avoiding Air Canada's fuel surtax on flights to and from Europe). This time, we thoroughly enjoyed our four-day tour of the Windy City, including a huge blues festival in the park with the Bean, a Cubs game in the legendary confines of Wrigley Field, the river tour, award-winning Chicago deep-dish pizza, and a performance of Hamilton on a downtown stage.

Family Christmas 2019. (Left to right: Gilad, Erin, me, Sheila, Mackenzie and Pierre. Not quite in photo is Kenz' pup Cali.)

Our trips to big cities have often featured live theatre, including Les Miserables in NYC, London, and Toronto; Lion King, also on Broadway; Miss Saigon, War Horse and Billy Elliott, also in London's West End; and Bring in Da Noise, Bring in Da Funk with our friends Dan and Shauney Denis from Prince George in an impromptu and unforgettable trip to San Francisco.

I have seen Les Miserables five or six times live, each with a different Jean Val Jean in the lead role (which I only wish I had the talent to play). All have been spectacular, but none more than the first time on Broadway, no less. We phoned in to try and get same-day tickets to the Phantom of the Opera. They were sold out, but the lady told me that she had great tickets come available for a show that was taking the city by storm. The seats were those normally held for royalty but had not been taken for this performance. From the centre of Row J, we saw a show that literally blew me away. And many years later, Les Miserables remains beyond comparison.

A few years later, we even saw Les Miserables performed on ice. It was the year-end performance of the Royal Glenora Skating Club, which that year featured world champions Kurt Browning and the tiny but immensely talented Kristi Yamaguchi. As if that wasn't enough, Michael Burgess, Canada's foremost musical theatre star, was brought in to sing "Bring Him Home" for Browning's solo performance. In an arena holding perhaps 200 people, I will never forget either Burgess nor the crisp sounds of Browning's skates on the ice. We felt so lucky to be there.

In costume to introduce performance of Man of La Mancha at Citadel Theatre.

I had met Burgess once before when I was the emcee for a special charity performance of Man of la Mancha at Edmonton's Citadel Theatre. We had the whole cast join the audience for a catered reception afterwards. I was expecting the actors to make token appearances, but I underestimated the appeal of free food and drinks. Erin told me later that she loved dancing at corporate gigs for that very reason.

Across the Pond, with the Marines

We have not only enjoyed visiting most countries in western Europe but also a couple of trips to Israel, which were expanded to include Cairo (the pyramids) and Istanbul for the markets and cross of Asian and European cultures. Israel is a great country to visit, and we later returned there for Erin's wedding. There were only about 10 of us there on behalf of the bride, but as my brother-in-law, Jeff said, "It was the most fun wedding ever." Not only were the food and hours of dancing wonderful, but even more so was the hospitality shown to us by Gilad's family, the Mizrahis. They are great people, and we are so proud to add Gilad, his three brothers, and their parents to our family, even if regular visits are not quite in the budget.

Our first trip to Europe came when Sheila's sister Ann was stationed in Belgium with her husband, Larry. They were on the SHAPE armed forces base there, which included many American military members. After a visit to London, we took a ferry across the strait from Dover to Calais. From there, we bussed to Lille - only about an hour's drive from where they lived in Belgium. They were great hosts, especially since Ann was not working and could take us all over, showing us castles and wineries that were more than 1,000 years old. Larry loved military history and provided us with personalized tours of the trenches and memorials from WWI and the fields of Waterloo, where I enjoyed a Napoleon-named local brew.

It was a great visit thanks largely to the hospitality of our hosts and the generosity of my parents for looking after Erin (who was about three at the time). But I think the story that I most like to tell was our day trip to Amsterdam. We were the only civilians on a bus full of U.S. Marines. We were fortunate to be only about two hours from many of the great cities in the world, including Paris, Frankfurt and Amsterdam, as well as other smaller but equally amazing places, such as the beautiful Bruges, with its amazing canals and chocolates.

The bus trip, largely through the countryside with wind turbines and the traditional windmills, was lovely, and Amsterdam is filled with wonders, including Anne Frank's house and art museums. But it was a conversation with one of the Marines on the trip home that I remember best.

Out of the blue, one rather muscular Marine asked me, "do I look gay to you?" I said, "No, not to me (before the time of the Seinfeld phrase, not that there's anything wrong with that)." He responded, "well, I must have to the guys in Amsterdam, as they were hitting on me everywhere I went." That in itself was perhaps not that surprising were it not for the fact that he was traveling with his wife, who was probably about eight months pregnant. Again, we were in the right place at the right time for a great experience.

There were other times we were fortunate to be in places at not the wrong time. We were in New Orleans just prior to Hurricane Katrina, NYC a week or so before 9/11, and in the roller coaster at West Edmonton Mall a few days before a fatal crash. We were also in Edmonton during its tragic tornado in 1987. We were totally unaware of what was happening, other than a torrent of rain. Sheila was driving in the car with baby Erin only about a few miles away from the tornado when it hit. We also felt an earthquake in Hawaii but were far enough from the epicentre to not witness any damage.

However, things do tend to happen to us (usually me) when we are on holiday, and Hawaii was no exception. The flight there stopped for fueling and supplies in Vancouver. It was unseasonably cold there, even for mid-December, and I think I got a chill in my back, which was iffy at the best of times, especially on a long flight. Whatever the reason, the next day, warm and sunny in Oahu, I could barely get out of bed or walk - the pain in my lower back was so severe (I blamed it on walking on flip flops on the beach the night before).

It was the first day of our holiday (essentially our honeymoon), and I could not function - even to walk one tiny step at a time. When I could not find a phone listing for a chiropractor within walking distance in Honolulu, I booked an appointment for acupuncture instead. I had received treatments from chiropractors and physios at home, and this seemed like an interesting adaptation, only using needles. I am not sure the treatment helped, but the practitioner also gave me a prescription for a muscle relaxer.

Sheila was about to catch the next flight home, but we decided to get at least a little beach time first. And this is where the story gets interesting. I took my baby steps towards the beach, looking for any wheelchair ramp and was being passed even by 80-year-olds. I finally made it to a change room to put on my bathing suit. Unfortunately, I accidentally dropped my suit on the floor of the room and could not bend down to pick it up. Others changing looked strangely at me, but nobody offered to help, so I tried picking up my suit with my toes - and eventually succeeded.

I walked gingerly out to the beach with Sheila wondering what took me so long - and then I lost hold of my underpants, which fell in the sand. On the sand, it was even more difficult to retrieve my fallen garment, and within seconds a circle of people formed around me to watch the show. Eventually, I picked up my gotchies by which time Sheila had come back to get me.

Once I started taking the pills, my back pain eased up, and I could lay by the pool - although I could not enjoy the dollar Mai Tais being offered.

Don't Cry for Me Argentina

I think equally funny and unusual was our first trip to Puerto Vallarta, and my encounter with an eel. We were on holiday with Sheila's brother Gordon and his wife, Marsha.

Hamming it up for a photo in Mexico.

Gord is a great guy and a real character. He loved the nickname "El Gordo" given to him by the local kids, as he carried a bit of extra padding around the middle. We had a lot of laughs, but the biggest ones came on the beach heading back to our hotel after an afternoon of beach volleyball, which is not as easy as it looks. It is hard to run or jump in the sand or to see serves purposely launched high into the bright Mexican sun.

On the walk down the beach, we had seen the skeleton of a moray eel, eaten away by the birds, but nevertheless nasty looking. We later learned that the eels like to move into the rocky areas near the shore at dusk. However, it was at that time that Marsha decided to go out for a swim. I walked a ways out to keep an eye on her when I felt something bite into my ankle. I tried to shake it loose. It had a good grip, but eventually, let go.

I yelled as I limped in over the rocks to the shore, bleeding from my ankle. Gordon wrapped my ankle with his bandana, and Marsha found some sort of dolly, which they used to wheel me back to our hotel.

I remember a couple of American twins, blondes (what else?), speculating if I would ever walk again (a similar comment, also from blonde twins in Toronto, when I had broken my ankle).

A Mexican doctor attended to me. As he squeezed out any possible poisons and applied some type of ointment, I yelped, and he started singing, "Don't Cry for Me Argentina." Gordon, Marsha, and Sheila, all who had been quite helpful to that point, could not stop laughing. A day or so later, we would meet the same doctor having a drink at Senor Frogs - still a popular hangout in PV. He told us of his medical training in Houston and how we were lucky to be able to visit the beaches of Mexico for two weeks a year, while he was "in paradise" all year long. After 65 winters in Canada, I can't say I disagree.

Gordon also had his issues with the unusual street smells in Mexico, especially the exhaust from the old diesel buses. One day, his stomach could take it no longer, and he stopped over a bridge to empty its contents into the stream below. In so doing, he threw up right on a group of seagulls. They were not happy at all about this, but we figured it was only fitting given how many people they must have pooped down on over the years.

The Littlefairs

Unfortunately, Sheila's mom Joyce died a year before I met Sheila, but I did get to know her dad Jim quite well before he died. My brother called him "Spence" as, with his tight curly white hair, he reminded him of Spencer Tracy. He was quite a guy and the father of nine children, all of whom turned out to be good people.

I have already mentioned several of Sheila's siblings - Ann, Ruth, Wendy, and Gordon. But I wouldn't be forgiven if I did not complete the listing with the rest of the boys: David, Barry, Ian, and last but not least, Tony - the youngest. They are quite a family and even more so when you add on spouses and children.

Gordon and Marsha, by the way, are no longer married but are still friends - and friends with us as well. Among other lasting legacies, they brought up two lovely young women - Brittany and Danielle.

My next couple of stories feature Brittany. The first is a line Brit knows I am saving for her wedding. One day, in her backyard, pretty little Brittany let go an enormous belch. Uncle Tom asked her, "what do you say, Brit?" expecting the usual "excuse me." Clearly, her father's daughter, she immediately responded, "ripper!"

Many years later, with Gordon and Marsha living in the U.S., Brittany came to visit us in Prince George, along with her cousin Rebecca, Steve, and Wendy's youngest of two daughters. One day, I decided to take Brit, Becky, and Mackenzie with me to the driving range. I was down in the lower section, hitting my driver, and they were upstairs hitting irons.

However, as it happened, Rebecca hit more than an iron as her backswing slashed open a sizable cut over Brittany's eye. She was bleeding profusely, so I took her to the hospital where I worked. It was a good thing that they knew me there as folks in the ER stitched her up quickly even though Brit came in with no healthcare insurance. As I said, she is Gordon's daughter, so why would one expect her to travel with insurance? Brit remains seemingly unscarred - although she has not taken to golfing as a past-time.

Brittany was actually one of 10 Canadians to come to Israel for Erin's wedding, and we took a day trip together into Palestine to meet there with some social workers, whom Brittany had connected with prior to our trip. It was an eye-opening trip to a world we had only seen through the eyes of American media. We saw both despair and triumph of the human spirit as these people set out to help children dealing with disabilities to get an education and learn to survive in a difficult world around them.

Sheila and I are Godparents to Wendy and Steve's daughters, Rebecca and Andrea. They are close to the same ages as our daughters and have always been close friends. My favourite Becky story, which I was able to tell at her wedding, came when she was still a baby. One night, during the 1988 summer Olympics, I was asked to babysit Becky, who was still in diapers and on formula. With Canadian sprinter Ben Johnson scheduled to run in the 100 metre final that night, I was not going out so saw no reason not to stay home with Becky.

With Johnson in the starting blocks, Becky launched a projectile of formula over me and onto the carpet. I told her, "sorry Becky, but you're going to have to wait 10 seconds before I can clean this up." Johnson won the gold medal and set a world record of 9.79 seconds. However, both were ultimately taken from him when he tested positive for performance-enhancing drugs. The medal was gone, but the story remains (I had actually met a less powerful version of Johnson years earlier covering amateur sports. He was a Jamaican immigrant with a bad stutter who only wanted to make good and never asked for the pedestal on which he was hoisted and from which he so dramatically fell).

Also traveling to Israel was Tony's oldest son Ryan, an engineer, who Sheila always says bears a strong resemblance to tennis star Rafael Nadal and movie star Tom Cruise. She, of course, pointed this out to Erin's mother-in-law, Tsiyona, while at their house for Shabbat dinner. She took a liking to Ryan, calling him Tom Cruise. A delightful lady and warm host, Tsiyona's grasp of English was not quite as strong as that of her husband or sons, and she later exclaimed, "I think Tom Cruise is boring (meaning bored)."

Ryan also came up with a memorable line of his own years earlier when his mother Shelley sent him to the door of our new house in the Edmonton suburb of Lansdowne. Greeting him at the door was our friend and Highballer teammate, Smitty (Dave Smith), with a young Mackenzie. Shelley subsequently asked him if it was the right house, and Ryan responded, "I don't know, but they have a new dad."… We always have had a "Smitty's room" wherever we have lived, as he comes to stay from time to time, and now house and dog-sits for us when we go on vacation. I could probably write at least a chapter of just Smitty stories, but I will not steal his glory, as he is, among other things, a published photo-journalist.

Day 10: In Alberta, the number of COVID-19 cases continues to increase at much the same pace, with 486 diagnosed to start the day. Numbers are proportionately similar across Canada, where many people are now in isolation at home, and governments are trying to find ways to ease the economic burden. Internationally, China, where it originated, is now well past its worst, with almost all new cases being their citizens returning from other infected countries. However, the United States, which was slow to react, now has more diagnosed cases than any other country, and they are nowhere near their peak. On a more positive front, many companies have converted some of their production to much-needed medical supplies, and people are finding creative ways to entertain themselves and others, from a social distance.

Entertaining House Guests

We have almost always had a spare room and welcomed guests. In Edmonton, these guests have largely consisted of visiting family, friends, and sometimes friends of friends. Often the visits are just for a few days and sometimes longer, particularly for students, short of cash and very appreciative. We are happy to help and, most of the time, enjoy the company.

My mom was the same way as guests were always welcome. However, in some cases, they would wear out that welcome. Such was the story of Yoko, an engineer, who had a single room next to mine at Queen's. One time when my folks came down from Toronto for a visit, Yoko made my mom a cup of coffee. She was very appreciative and told him that if he was ever in the neighbourhood to stop by. Yoko obviously took note, as several years later, with my parents now in Calgary and me in Manitoba, he stopped by for a visit and stayed a couple of months. He even asked my sister Janet if she would like to go to her prom with him - a thought that horrified her.
Some of our most interesting house guests joined us when we lived in Prince George. With my job (ED of the hospital foundation) and none of us knowing a soul when we arrived there, we became very active members of the community. At least once a year, we hosted a Japanese student, a professional actress performing at Theatre NorthWest, and guests of my Rotary Club.

The Japanese students were about 17 and came to improve their English and learn about Canada. We always chose to host a boy. I actually don't recall which boy was which, but they were all very polite and appreciative. And for the sake of brevity, I will roll a couple of their experiences together under the name Hiroshi, who I think was our first student.

Two of the requirements for each student were to bring gifts from his or her family and to prepare a Japanese-style meal for us. We looked forward to each occasion. Every year, they also took trips to Jasper, which they liked, and the old west town of Barkerville, which they did not. Jasper's scenery is stunning and always attracts many Japanese visitors. The history of Barkerville had far less appeal, perhaps because our history is so recent compared to that in Japan.

However, our most memorable times were those unscheduled. One year, I was out of town for the first day of our student's arrival, and Sheila picked him up. That in itself threw him for a loop as it would not have been in the job description for wives in Japan. It amazed him even more when she popped up the double garage door with her car remote. Such space was also not common in Japan, and so he assumed we were rich (even though it was not us out spending huge amounts of money to buy Michael Jordan basketball shoes).

The fascination with space extended to the lawn. One day, he was outside as I was preparing to mow the front lawn. In a Tom-Sawyer-like move (re. painting the fence), I asked him if he would like to try. I thought I had a good thing going until a few minutes later after he had finished cutting our smallish front lawn. I asked him if he would like to do the backyard. "No. Very tired," he said.

One evening, he joined our slo-pitch team but was also surprised to see women playing with men on the same team. Another evening, we took him to an outdoor musical theatre performance. The show was good, but the weather was cold, and we had to put a blanket over us. I asked him if he liked the show. He said, "Yes, but like winter in Jah-Pan."

Unfortunately, the program was not a true exchange, and we long ago lost touch with our Japanese guests. We would have loved to have had them show us some of their country.

Golf Course in Siberia

Probably the most interesting of our Rotary guests were university professors from Siberia. I think we hosted three: a married couple of physics professors and a female professor/pediatrician. They were essentially there to see how service clubs worked in North America as there was no such tradition of them under Soviet rule.

My most vivid recollection of their stay was having them join us in a round of golf for the first time. I was playing with the husband while his wife was in the foursome behind. One hole, we held back a minute to see her approach shot into the green from approximately 60 yards away. Damned if she didn't sink it.

She lept in the air, screaming with joy. And he said, "I am going to start golf course in Siberia." We have not followed up to see if that happened, but I am sure it was the highlight of their visit.

We also enjoyed playing host to visiting actresses performing at our professional theatre. Every one was a different experience, but each loved acting and needed another job to make a living. One said to me, "I loved being on stage, but even when I've got a gig, I could earn more working at Safeway." It became a familiar story for us, as Erin also trained hard for many years to do something she loved for very low wages.

Probably my favourite actress was Donna Lea from Vancouver. She was a vibrant young lady who loved to spend time with our girls and one day invited the whole cast of A Christmas Carol to our house to do Christmas crafts. She also had a grandmother named Mabel and a husband who made us the best meat stew I've ever had.

However, the most unusual guest was a young woman from Toronto. She actually arrived on the evening of September 10, 2001, and, tired from her trip, did not have much of a chance to chat with us that night. By the next morning, the world had changed. We were actually watching The Today Show from NYC when the planes hit the towers. I could not see leaving for work without letting her know what had happened, so I woke her. Immediately, without knowing anything about it, she said that the Americans "deserved it."

She was a nice enough person but seemed to be experimenting with everything - vegan diet, lesbian/bisexual lifestyle, and playing the guitar. The guitar playing was fine, although she ended up leaving with Smitty's guitar, but the vegan diet was new to us, as was having a new female friend spend the night with her. Everybody's free to follow their own path, but trying every new path while staying with strangers was perhaps pushing the boundaries a bit more than we were expecting.

Do You Come from a Large Family?

I have had quite a few differing jobs in my career. Each had their satisfying moments as, for the most part, I was doing things that I enjoyed and got reasonably good at doing. However, by far the most gratifying component of each were the people with whom I worked - many of whom I still am friends with to this day.

Nowhere was this more true for me than Prince George, as I got to know a lot of people there, including those working with me at the Foundation.

My favourite story was the hiring of Nycole Ross as our administrative assistant. Elaine Smith had left the position, and Nycole was on a very short list when I brought her in for a second interview, which went like this:

"Welcome back, Nycole. I have brought you in for a second interview, but I actually only have one question. Do you come from a large family?"

"What?" she exclaimed vociferously. "You can't ask me that. Do you ask me because I am French Canadian and Catholic?"

"No," I said. "I ask you because you are talking so loud. My wife comes from a large family, and they are used to having to yell over each other. If you can take it down a notch and stop yelling, the job is yours."

Nycole not only took the job but stayed for many years, even after I moved back to Edmonton. And most times, she did manage to keep her voice down... except when speaking to her family in French on the phone. I should give her a call, as I miss hearing her voice.

Prince George Foundation staff dressed up as the Flintstones and I, as Fred, took my turn in the dunk tank.

She's the One I Lie To

I used to try and add summer students to the staff when government subsidies were available. They had new skills and also brought new life to an office, usually resulting in older staff to start dressing more fashionably to keep up.

Rachelle and Tobi in Prince George were two of the best - smart, hardworking, and a pleasure to have in the office. I thoroughly enjoyed engaging them in arguments, often just to get them going. It was fun, and I think of benefit to all, as Rachelle carried on working for several years in fund development, and Tobi went on to a successful career with the RCMP.

I will also highlight one young man at an NGO in Edmonton. He was from Jamaica, but it always amazed me that the dialect only came out when he was speaking to one of his buddies from back home. He dressed very sharply and was apparently quite the ladies' man. One day, overhearing a bit of his conversation, I asked him to whom he was talking as the tone sounded a little more tame than usual. He said, "oh, she's the one I lie to."

He explained that he didn't bother to lie or cover up with most of his lady friends, but this one he cared about, at least enough to lie to her about his goings-on. I pledged then that if I ever wrote a book that I would include that line.

Another interesting young man competed in bodybuilding championships. His hands were bright orange from all the carrots consumed, and the microwave usually smelled of broccoli. A few of us went to watch him in a competition for which he had been training. He was dark from the oils all over him and looked pretty impressive. However, he only finished fourth in his weight group. I asked him if he was disappointed. He said, "not at all. We all know that at least two of them will fail the drug test." Each to their own, I guess.

Day 11: The number of diagnosed COVID-19 cases in Alberta has risen to 542, but it seems that people do get used to almost anything, and things seem somewhat stable, despite the pervasive impacts of the pandemic. On the home front, we are still in isolation for a few more days but are healthy and not yet totally crazy. And this book is proceeding on schedule, with just another day or two of writing left to finish.

Near-Death Experiences

As described earlier, I was informed by doctors that I died three years ago from a heart event, only to survive and recover - such that I can write this book.

However, I have narrowly escaped death several times in my life. Fortunately, I guess it was just not my time. I am here to tell the tales, in somewhat random order as it is hard to measure, which were actually my closest calls. But the following are a selection of tales, as close to fact as I can recall:

Undoubtedly, the scariest incident was when I literally stared death in the face and walked away unscathed. I was driving from Portage to Calgary with my friend Ian Smith, who also went by Smitty. It was dark, and we were only about two hours from Calgary on the TransCanada Highway, just past Medicine Hat. It is a hilly stretch but, at the time, just one lane each way. I went to pass a car, but it sped up and would not let me by as we hit the hill. Going full speed, I was parallel to the other car when I suddenly faced headlights right before me. It was so close that I could read the brand name of his vehicle from the car hood. I had no chance to get into the right lane, so steered directly in front of the oncoming vehicle and onto his shoulder. I hit ice there and went down into a ditch.

I knew that my quick reactions had saved us from instant death and felt, in a strange way, exhilarated by the experience. However, poor Smitty was as white as a sheet, for he too saw his life pass before him.

The car we were trying to pass never did stop, but the one coming towards us came back and helped haul us out of the ditch. He said, "I was half asleep and froze when I saw your lights right in front of me. I am sure glad you reacted the way you did. Otherwise, we would both have died right there."

I have gone off the road a few times, but that was the closest to a life-ending experience. Another time, I fell asleep at the wheel driving from Portage to Winnipeg, perhaps the straightest drive in the country. The road and traffic were fine, but the sun shone directly into my eyes and I twice I woke up when the car went on the shoulder. When I got to Winnipeg, I was obviously still half asleep as I drove up the entrance ramp. With headlights again coming my way, I backed up and continued on my way. I don't text or drink and drive, but disabled driving can come in many forms, and I don't fare well with the sun in my eyes.

In another instance, I was driving home to Prince George from a work meeting in Quesnel, about an hour's drive south. By the time I headed back, it was pitch black and snowing heavily. If you have had to drive in such conditions, you probably know that the snow in the lights of the vehicle can be mesmerizing, as well as limiting to one's visibility. I don't know whether I fell asleep momentarily or just glanced down at my car instruments, but somehow I missed a sharp turn. Next thing I knew, my Windstar was rolling and flipping off the road. It was a weird feeling as it was like time was almost suspended, and I was flipping in slow motion. When it stopped, I was hanging upside down from my seat belt. I was not hurt at all and was able to undo the belt, open the door and climb out.

I called the BCAA, which hauled my car back to its wheels. From there, I was actually able to drive home and parked the car in the driveway. When Sheila got home, she saw the car, which looked worse than it was, and asked what had happened. I said, "you're not going to ask if I'm okay?" She responded. "I can see you're okay from the silly smile on your face." I felt lucky to have walked out of the accident without injury, as it could easily have ended much worse.

Another head-on was not with a vehicle but rather a long box. I was practicing my vaulting but failed to lift my head in time and ran full speed into the wooden box. I was not diagnosed, but am pretty sure that it was my first concussion - and the end of my short-lived service to the gymnastics team.

My first diagnosed concussion came while tobogganing with friends on the slopes by Government House in Edmonton. I flipped, hit my hit on the ice, and then had the sled land on my head. I was told that I asked the same questions repeatedly, and the emergency doctor confirmed that I was concussed. Oddly enough, at about the same time, and within a mile or so of my accident, my Sun colleague Scott Haskins was also injured - hit by a car near Teddy's bar on Jasper. He had been there, then turned around when crossing the street to go back and look at a car in Edmonton Motors. Our editor was not impressed.

In other close calls, I escaped unharmed when I bounced with my hand off the side of a moving truck and then a railway overpass, when riding my bike to Junior High in Toronto, and I nearly fell down a cliff during a high school trip to Greece. I was climbing and used a root for a hand-grip. The root came out, and I fell back. No harm done but I was just one step from falling down a steep, rocky cliff.

I have also had many various illnesses, including bouts of bronchitis and pneumonia, mononucleosis, a suspected but undiagnosed case of H1N1 (which scared me as I could not catch my breath), and kidney stones. My second bout of kidney stones actually came when I was still in bed from my heart event. I did not know what was happening and initially thought it was my back complaining about my recent heart event. It was not until I got home, and the pain got very intense that Sheila took me to emergency with a suspected kidney stone.

They did some tests which they said they would send to a urologist and sent me home. I waited a few days but got no call, and when we (Wendy, a unit clerk at U of A hospitals) checked with the hospital, we found out that their fax had not worked. However, eventually, I saw the urologist who confirmed kidney stones but was not sure what to do, given my recent heart event. He ultimately decided that surgery was the best option as the pain from the kidney stones was too threatening to my heart.

He told me, "I have operating time at the Alex (Royal Alexandra Hospital) tonight. Go right now and, unless there is a shooting there, I will do the surgery tonight."
So we proceeded to the Alex, and I got prepped for surgery. However, it was delayed and delayed, eventually to the next morning. Sure enough, some guy had shot a cop and bumped me out of my slot in emergency surgery.

Only If You Win the Nobel Peace Prize

I have enjoyed telling you some of the stories from things that have happened to me but have left out more than I have written, including many interesting characters

Tales to Tell My Daughters

whom I have met along the way.

Perhaps the most unusual and interesting is (Dr.) Austin Mardon. He has authored or co-written more than 130 books, so I will not seek to retell his stories, but I would like to share a couple of them, which I also experienced.

Firstly, for those who don't know him, Austin is a very large man. He recently lost about 100 pounds but is still close to 400 pounds and is 6'5. He also has a white beard, reminding one of Farley Mowat. Also, and most notably, he has lived with schizophrenia for many years, and it was through mental health advocacy that we met, some 10 to 12 years ago.

Austin gets easily bored, and for the past few years, I have found my way on to his A-list for calling, which he does once or twice a day. Often, he is just calling to kill time but, perhaps because he is a friend or perhaps in deference to concerns about his schizophrenia, I almost always will either take or return the call. However, I have had to set ground rules in terms of the time of day - with no calls before 0800 and none after 2100.

Austin almost always keeps his calls within that time frame. I have pointed out that although I am usually up by 0600, I don't want to be phoned that early. I also now go to bed at 10, so nine seemed to be a reasonable cutoff at the end of the day.

One morning Austin phoned and asked me if I knew what day it was. "Tuesday, I think, why?" I answered. "No," he said, "it's the day they announce the winners of the Nobel Peace Prize. You know that I am nominated, right?"

I acknowledged that he had told me of the nomination but pointed out that it is normally given to people of world acclaim, like Nelson Mandela.

He continued, "but can I call you? It will be about three in the morning here." I said, "yes, Austin, you can call me if you win, but if you call me to tell me that you didn't win, then you are cut off from calling."

I have received calls from Austin saying that he was to be given the Order of Canada, the Canadian Medical Association (CMA) medal of honour, and honorary doctorates from the University of Alberta and University of Lethbridge; but I still await the call for the Nobel Peace Prize. After all, when it comes to Austin, an accomplished man and one of the greatest self-promoters ever, who knows?

Austin's wife Catherine is also a remarkable woman - a former American lawyer who was almost stabbed to death for her efforts by the Klu Klux Klan. Her injuries have also caused her mobility issues, so she does not fly often. So when it came to receiving his CMA medal in St. John's, Nfld., Austin asked if I would like to be his guest. I had only been to the Rock once on a golf trip with Frank and Jamie. I welcomed the chance to go again - and on somebody else's dime. I phoned my friend Alex, a business prof at Memorial University, to let him know that I would be coming his way with a special guest.

The trip down from Edmonton was uneventful, as was the conference itself. I saw my role there being largely to remind Austin that he was not the schizophrenic superhero that the docs and some of the families made him out to be. Austin is very human, but I realized that compared to the average person with schizophrenia, his achievements were beyond belief.

Beyond the ongoing work to advocate for those with mental illness for which he was most recognized, Austin had also managed to go on an Antarctic expedition, be arrested by the KGB in Moscow, and as mentioned, author, co-author, or edit, more than 130 books and countless academic papers. He was no ordinary fellow, regardless of his mental illness.

Aside from the mental illness, Austin also had some physical disability, partly from his weight and partly from frostbite in his feet suffered in Antarctica. Walking was a challenge for him, but I did not travel all the way to St. John's to sit in a hotel room or conference rooms. I like to walk, and prior to my heart event, usually did so at a fair clip.

One trip was to Quidi Vidi (pronounced Kitty Vitty), a quaint little fishing harbour and one of the most photographed sites in the St. John's area. There, Austin slipped a bit on the dock but, according to his story, he almost drowned in the Atlantic.
Another day, I convinced him to walk back to our hotel from the convention centre to see the legendary George Street, with its two blocks of back-to-bar bars and the shops down Water Street. In all, it was perhaps a one km stretch, but Austin needed to stop for coffee just about every block. Finally, only about 50 yards from the hotel, he said he could walk no further and wanted to take a cab. I told him that no cab would be willing to drive him 50 yards, so we stopped for another coffee and eventually made it the rest of the way.

However, the funniest story from that trip came on our flight home. Because of his size, Austin usually manages to get three seats set aside for two people. This time, however, the flight was packed, and a man sat down between us. He was a big guy - bigger than I was - although nowhere near as large as Austin. He was wearing a Harley Davidson leather jacket and ball cap.

Perhaps he was a decent guy, but things got off to a rough start even before we took off. For some unknown reason, the Air Canada staff made their initial announcements in not only English and French but also in Spanish.

Austin commented, "Why are they doing that?" The Harley guy, in the middle, apparently did not hear the Spanish and thought Austin was complaining about an announcement in French. He said to Austin, with a strong Francophone accent, "Do you have a problem with that?"

Austin immediately shut up and did not say a word or even move for the whole flight.

And Now He's our Prime Minister

I have saved my Justin Trudeau story for last. It may not be my best story, but given the times we are in now and the critical role of our Prime Minister in dealing with it, I thought it would be fitting - and perhaps give some insights into our leader.

I was asked by the national office of the Canadian Mental Health Association to represent it at a dinner recognizing donors to mental health. It was being held at the beautiful and stately Chateau Laurier Hotel in Ottawa. Wanting to save the organization some money, I booked into another hotel, where I had stayed before, just a few blocks away.

The event was being hosted by Sophie Gregoire, wife of Justin Trudeau, then a Liberal MP who was being considered for the party leadership. Sophie was not only a well-spoken TV personality but also was willing to speak to her own mental health challenges (no not those with Justin, ha ha) with eating disorders.

I went up to introduce myself, and she asked if I would like to meet her husband, Justin. I mentioned to him that I had met his dad years ago on the campaign trail in Manitoba and had met his mom, Margaret, a few times in her role as a spokesperson for mental health (I quite liked Margaret, but my mom didn't like her any more than she did Pierre).

I don't recall what Justin said, but I remember him to be both polite and charming, seeming to show interest in what I had to say.

A while later, the event ended, and I left the Chateau Laurier to go back to my hotel. It was pitch black and pouring rain, and I had exited from what I am sure was the furthest distance from the front of the hotel. By the time I had walked around the whole building, the only people to be seen were Sophie and Justin. I had crossed the street but waited at the light to extend greetings.

Justin did not wait for the light to change and ran across, in the dark and rain, in front of traffic, to come say hello, leaving Sophie standing at the light.

"Justin, what are you doing?" I said to him. "You just ran across the street in front of traffic and left your lovely wife standing there in the rain."

"Yes, sometimes I am not thinking," he said. The light changed, and Sophie then joined us. I pointed out her husband's conduct was somewhat lacking and said, "I think you can do better." She responded, "yes, sometimes, so do I."

Now Justin is our Prime Minister, trying to lead our country through a very difficult time. I do not know if Justin Trudeau is providing us with the best solutions, but I do think that my brief meeting was a reflection of the man - for better or for worse.

In Conclusion

That concludes the tales to be told in this venture. These are but a sampling of what could be told with many more there for the telling. Perhaps someday in the future, some of them will be put in writing - hopefully while I am still here to do the telling, and without a virus restriction providing the catalyst and time to write. In the meantime, I hope you have enjoyed reading "Tales to Tell My Daughters," and I look forward to your feedback.

Take care of yourself and each other,

-Tom (the dad)

Epilogue

Day 12 and 13: I am finished writing but have gone back to edit. The number of diagnosed cases in Alberta increased to 621, then 662, and a third person passed away. It is acknowledged that the number of infected would surely be higher except that people with mild symptoms are being asked to not take up the limited testing resources and just stay home in isolation.

Day 14: This is the last day of our self-isolation, and it comes just in time as now those in isolation have been told to not even leave their own properties. I can't see the harm in walking the dog around the block, but I guess that too many people have not limited themselves to that and have been getting close to others. The number of infected in Alberta has only risen marginally to 690, but the death toll has increased to eight, with many more people still at risk in ICUs. On the book front, I have also gone back for another round of editing. I am sure there are still things that I could clean up and an almost endless number of stories that could be added, but I think that I am done now, except for perhaps adding some photos.

CHAPTER THREE
BONUS STORIES

On request from my daughters, I am adding a few Shand family-oriented stories.

My parents both enjoyed music. Unfortunately, they were both tone-deaf. I am not aware that either gave any serious attempt at playing a musical instrument, but both did try to sing - my mom often boisterously. I don't recall hearing my dad's voice that often; although, in his last years at the old folks' home, I did go with him to the sing-songs when I was visiting. The old gals there encouraged him. I imagine they most were most likely quite hard of hearing and also hard up for some male companionship, as the ratio of women to men there was probably three to one.

My dad preferred the ladies with the 1950s beehive hairdos from the Lawrence Welk Show. I tried to tell him that those women were likely all long gone, or at least in their 90s now, but he still preferred them to the women he actually saw every day. I thought they presented themselves well, but he said, "I don't think they even looked good when they were young." I thought it was too bad that he didn't give some of those ladies a look, but I guess he still saw himself as the dashing young man that met my mom some 70 years earlier.

Growing up, we always had a piano in the house. We all tinkered on it, but the only one with the discipline to actually learn how to play properly was my sister, Janet. I think she ended up earning her Grade Eight. My parents encouraged her, but I think her skills were pretty much lost on them.

One day, I was in our living room in Toronto, and my dad was in the kitchen. He told me, "Janet's piano playing sounds pretty good, don't you think?" I had to tell him that it was our cat, Boots, walking up and down the piano keys. Those piano lessons really paid off.

83

Although my dad had grown up with dogs, my mom preferred cats, and so my parents didn't get a dog until they moved to Calgary in 1975. However, Boots, our cat, perhaps thought he was a dog. At least, I am not aware of that many cats stealing a pork chop right off a barbecue.

When my parents eventually got a dog, it was a beauty. Henry was a Springer Spaniel, and the grandson of what some books claimed was the greatest show dog of all time. Unfortunately, at least from the breeder's standpoint, Henry's ears weren't of show calibre, and so he became available for purchase. And with my mom training him largely on her own, his behaviour wasn't exactly show quality, either.

Henry was spoiled and very sensitive. He was great with people but did not like being left alone. It was not unusual for my parents to come home to a chewed up chair or drapes. It's too bad that my mom never passed her driver's test (putting the car in forward instead of reverse in attempting to leave the parking stall) as Henry could be left in the car for an hour and never wrecked a thing.

My brother and sister were in high school and then university during the time that Henry needed training. So it was left to my mom, who had no idea of how to train a dog. She loved Henry but complained about getting, and being left with, a dog. Henry was named after my dad whose middle name was Henry. Apparently, if he had been a girl, he would have been Henrietta (and I would not be here writing this story).

One day, my brother Jamie took Henry out for a walk along with our cousin Pam. Henry saw a rabbit and took off. The rabbit went under a fence, and Henry ran smack into it - and Jamie laughed. Henry collapsed, so Jamie picked him up and carried him home. When they got to the driveway, my mom called out to the dog. It jumped out of Jamie's arms and ran to her. No harm done but Jamie had hurt Henry's feelings by laughing at his folly.

My daughters always wanted a family dog as well, but we didn't give in until we moved to Prince George. Eventually, Sheila gave in and set up some conditions by which Mackenzie could get a dog. She and I would go to the SPCA once a week following her weekend dance class and would check out the dogs. One day, we came home with a pup - a mixed breed of some sort, which we named Maggie, which Sheila would sometimes extend to Maggie Mae.

As best we could guess, Maggie was at least partly a Staffordshire Terrier, as she had the thick neck and flattened features of a bull terrier, probably crossed with a yellow lab. She was a very loyal and loving dog, at least to all humans. We never knew her background, but we guessed she had some bad experiences as a young pup, as she would not set foot in the garage. When I took her for our first walk, I had to practically drag her as, based on her nails, I don't think she had been walked before.

We all loved Maggie, but nobody more than Mackenzie. One day, she called Sheila at work. She was just bawling, so Sheila had no idea what had happened.

A sobbing Mackenzie said, "Mom, you can't get rid of her, I love her so much." Sheila asked her what she was talking about. Kenz said, "Maggie tore a hole in the hot tub lid." Sheila asked, "How big? Was it bigger than a bread box, or a book?" Mackenzie responded, "what book?"

Unlike my parents' Henry, Maggie never chewed anything that wasn't hers in the house. But outdoors was a different story. And the small tear in the hot tub lid was no match for her powerful jaws. The hot tub lid was replaced, but Maggie was with us for many more years until cancer took her from us (I won't tell that story as it upsets Mackenzie too much).

A short while after Maggie passed, Mackenzie was home from university for a visit and could not bear for us to have no dog. So she and Sheila showed up in my office with a black ball of fur, which she named Coco, after Coco Chanel. She is a Golden Doodle but almost all black from the poodle genes. Kenz also now has her own dog - a gorgeous Golden Retriever named Cali.

Art Linkletter used to have a T.V. show, which featured a segment called "Kids Say the Darndest Things." My kids were no exception.

My favourite from Mackenzie was when we were listening to the national anthems on some sports broadcast. She exclaimed, indignantly, "It's not fair. They (Americans) have three national anthems, and we (Canadians) only have one." Sheila asked, "What three are they?" to which Mackenzie responded, "Oh Say Can You See, American the Beautiful, and Old Lang Syne," and then carried on to say that "And it's just not their land, you know," referring to "Our home and native land." Sheila still says, "I really miss Mackenzie. (Both of our daughters live far from Edmonton). She always makes me laugh."

We would be wise to listen more often to what our kids have to say, speaking words of wisdom. One day, we were driving out of Prince George when the radio host, Mike Benny, said, "don't touch that dial." Erin asked, in all earnestness, "Dad, what's a dial?" I gave Mike a call and explained to him that kids nowadays aren't familiar with a dial.

85

Within a minute, we heard Mike relay to his radio audience that he had just heard from a listener that he was dated in his remarks and explained the past use of a dial to our remote control/Bluetooth generation.

Formal family photo shortly after move to Prince George.

Erin also called a mouse under her pillow at a rural hotel in Athabasca "Oh little Mickey Mouse" as her mom and a friend screamed and jumped up on the other bed. And she referred to spicy rice dishes as "nanny food" as one of her friends had a Filipino nanny.

We had actually bought our house in Prince George from Mike. He was a well-respected radio personality but not so much of a handyman. We were in a corner house, so we only had a neighbour on one side, with sidewalks to shovel and lawn to mow on the side and back of the property. Across the street was a little Fijian man who was constantly urging me to install built-in sprinklers outside of my fence, as he didn't like when that lawn got brown or rough looking. I, of course, blamed Mike for not extending the sprinkler system to that area. I told the Fijian man that if he wanted to pay for the sprinkler extension, I would agree to the extra lawn mowing that it would cause. He kindly declined my offer but still didn't like the brown lawn.

Tales to Tell My Daughters

One day I was out digging out an old garden to put in a paved area for basketball. My Fijian friend showed up behind me, curious as to what I was up to. While he was there, I stepped on an old nail that went right through my running show and stuck in my foot.

I pulled the nail out, but my neighbour was quite concerned. "You know where I came from?" he said. "Same village in Fiji as V.J. Singh (the golfer). One day a man in our village stepped on a nail. Next day he was dead... Next day, he was dead."

Although I never followed his advice when it came to expanding our sprinkler system, I did head his warming and got a tetanus shot.

In our family, I think the funniest lines came from my brother Jamie, particularly when he was young. I have already told the story of this little kid, maybe six at the time, telling my dad that "Grandpa and Gertrude (a busy woman who he remarried after my grandmother died) are out in the boat - necking."

Around that time and also in cottage country, we were touring Stephen Leacock's home in Orillia, north of Toronto. The tour guide, likely a summer job for a university student, told us that everything in the house was as it had been when Leacock lived there. Jamie threw her for a loop when he asked if they were the original logs in the fireplace.

He would also correct store clerks for not entering groceries correctly on the till. He was always good with numbers and could complete the math puzzles in the Globe and Mail while still in elementary school.

I think one of the funniest stories came when we were on a family vacation to Washington, D.C. and stopped for lunch at a diner in Virginia. Our waitress asked what we would like to eat, and young Jamie said, "Kentucky Fried Chicken." The waitress was charmed and exclaimed in her most extreme southern Black accent, "this is Virginia, honey. If you would care for some Virginia fried chicken, I would be most obliged to bring you some."

My sister Janet was always deemed to be the good daughter, who didn't get into as much trouble as her brothers. However, she was very deceiving and often the underlying troublemaker, particularly around Jamie, who would be told off for laughing in church or in the middle of somebody's story at the dinner table. One night at dinner, my dad got so annoyed that he lost it and threw a plastic Ketchup bottle at me. It missed, but the lid came off on impact with the wall, and there was red everywhere. At least this time, it was Janet who was sent to her home, albeit with a smile on her face.

With my dad and Jamie, dressed up for his wedding.

Janet went on to the University of Alberta and became a registered nurse, first in hospitals and then homecare. One of her earliest patients came from a tackle football game in our backyard when she was probably eight or nine years old. My friend Dieter, a big kid from school, was hit hard and was in pain on the ground. He called out for a drink, and Janet ran in the house to help. However, it seemed like forever until she returned - with a large glass of chocolate milk (from Nestle Quik powder) that she had taken the time to mix.

I am three and a half years older than Janet and six and a half years older than Jamie. I was at University at Queen's for most of their high school years (in Toronto and Calgary). However, one year when I was working in Manitoba, I came back to pick up Jamie at the end of his first year at U of A to drive him back to Calgary. When I got to his residence, it looked like there had been a riot. There were T.V.s, mattresses, and everything you could imagine tossed on the front lawn. I asked one of the students if Jamie Shand was anywhere around and was told, "Oh, you mean, Animal? He got out of here before the police arrived."

The next year, Jamie moved in with some friends from Calgary into an off-campus apartment building. It was an incredible mess, even when I went to visit. I'm sure the same Oreos were on the floor from my previous time there. A couple of their girlfriends were equally disgusted as they somehow got their hands on stationery from the health authorities and sent the boys a letter threatening eviction for not complying with health standards. The ploy worked, although only once.

On further request and recollections, I am adding a few more of my favourite stories.

Planes, Trains, and Automobiles

I love the 80s movie Planes, Trains, and Automobiles, starring John Candy and Steve Martin. It is in one of three comedies in my top 10, with the other two being "Being There" and "Return of the Pink Panther," both starring the brilliant Brit Peter Sellers. I was going to include an appendix with some top 10 lists (movies, actors, musicians, albums, books, movie stars, T.V. shows, etc.;) but it seemed a little self-indulgent so unless there is demand you may have to indulge my slipping in these occasional references.

When our family moved to Prince George, it meant many trips back and forth to Alberta, where many of our relatives and friends lived. Prince George is basically in the middle of nowhere or in the centre of the western Canadian universe, depending on how you look at it. It is about an eight-hour drive to Vancouver, Prince Rupert, Calgary, or Edmonton. Over our more than 10 years in P.G., we did each of those drives often and occasionally had others come to see us. "The road does go both ways," Sheila used to remind some of those inclined to have us do almost all of the visiting.

There are not many stopping spots en route, particularly on the B.C. side of the border. Pretty much the only place to stop before you reached Jasper was the town of McBride. It is not a big town and had, true or not, the reputation of having hillbillies in its backwoods, with all that word's connotations. It is about a 150-minute drive from P.G. and another 90 minutes to Jasper. We seldom went into the town but almost always stopped at one of the two gas stations on the highway. I liked the one best on the west side as it had really good oatmeal and raisin cookies. It was a sad day when the supplier cut off the cookies there.

On one trip, when Mackenzie was very young, we were heading south (I think to pick up Erin at a meeting place in Jasper, as she had been visiting her cousins in Edmonton). We stopped for cookies and a washroom break at the gas station in McBride and left Kenz sleeping under a blanket in the back seat. When we pulled back onto the highway, Sheila spotted a little girl on the median of the highway and said, "that looks a lot like Mackenzie." Sure enough, she had come looking for us. Good thing Sheila was a good spotter, or Kenz might have joined one of the hillbilly clans.

Another time, we were heading to Calgary for Easter weekend and were having trouble with our Windstar. We checked into the hotel on the east side of the highway in McBride and asked the clerk if the service station just down the road would be open the next morning. He said yes, so we settled down for the night.

The next morning, I walked the 50 yards or so down to the station while Sheila and Kenz went for breakfast, and Erin stayed in the room to get a bit more sleep. When I got to the station, I asked if it was open, and the guy there said, "My mechanic will be here in about half an hour. He should be able to help you."

So I walked back to the room, intending to pick up Erin and get some breakfast. Erin told me that a guy from the gas station called and wanted me to come back.

So I turned around and headed back and saw the same guy. I said, "I thought you said the mechanic wouldn't be in for half an hour." He replied, "I am the mechanic."

When we checked out an hour or so later, I told the hotel clerk of my experience at the gas station. He told me, "Yeah, sorry about that. I should have mentioned something to you. He's a little strange, but it's the only place open here, and he is a pretty good mechanic."

The Windstar had a few neuro issues of its own. It served us well but had the odd electrical eccentricity. One time, I was out with my brother-in-law Steve (technically Sheila's brother-in-law) in the Windstar in Edmonton. When we stopped, the van's door locks started going up and down on their own. Steve asked me, "Did you do that?" and I asked him the same. "That felt like Poltergeist," he said. It stopped just as it had started, without explanation.

Winter driving can be extremely hazardous, and unfortunately, I have done far more than my share. On one trip, I made it fine until I hit a snowstorm around Hinton. I was eager to reach Edmonton and, with the rest of the drive on the double highway, was not wanting to pull over. I was having trouble seeing as the windshield wipers couldn't shake the build-up of ice. So, while driving down the highway, I opened my window to grab the wiper to free the ice. Instead, it freed the wiper, which flew off from my grasp. It seemed like forever before I reached Edson, as I stopped several times to hand wipe my windshield with snow. Fortunately, there was an auto parts store open in Edson, and the rest of my trip was uneventful.

The Matrix

Of the vehicles I have owned, I think I grew most attached to my Toyota Matrix. When it comes to cars, I have always been one to put function in front of form. And the Matrix ticked off pretty much all of the boxes for me. Inexpensive, great on gas, and lots of room, especially with the hatchback.

I bought it new in 2005, shortly after moving back to Edmonton. I had never owned a Toyota, but the brand had come a long way since Toyota's early days, and I was pulled in by a billboard promoting its price of less than $19,000.

Of course, when I went into the dealership, they tried hard to upgrade me to one with more features, such as power locks, automatic transmission, and air conditioning. The salesperson told me that "no one in Alberta buys the base model, only people in Quebec and Manitoba." I responded that the "extra cost for those extra features was about the same as a year of university for my daughters - and it is seldom hot enough to need air conditioning in Edmonton." He said that the features would help with resale, but when I told him that I fully expected to have the car for at least 10 years, he backed off and settled for the sale with less commission. He had to order the base model from the assembly line in Ontario, but I felt like I had won the battle. It was not until about 10 years later and I was rear-ended by a truck driver on his cell phone that I parted ways with my Matrix (I was on my way to a round of golf. I had to pull my clubs out through the back seat but still managed to make it in time for my golf game).

Prior to our Matrix, our smaller car was a Honda - also a hatchback. On one trip, we were heading to Edmonton for my father-in-law's memorial service. I was driving down a steep hill near McBride when I found myself with no control of the car in the ice slush. I told everybody to make sure their seat belts were secure. I eventually slid off the road rather than into oncoming traffic. Within minutes, a logging truck stopped, attached a chain, and pulled us out of the ditch, as if we were a toothpick. For once, we were thankful for sharing the road with big trucks.

On another trip, not in the winter and just a little further down the same stretch of road, we were having some transmission problems with the Civic. We were just able to make it to Mount Robson when the car would go no further. Fortunately, with all of our travel, we have been longtime users of AMA/BCAA. So we called for a tow, anticipating going to Valemount and renting a car there to complete our trip to Edmonton.

When the tow truck driver arrived, I asked him to just drive us to Valemount, the nearest town with any services. "Aren't you going to Edmonton?" he asked. "Sure," I said. "I'll just rent a car in Valemount and pick up this car in a few days."

"And who are you going to rent from?" he asked. "It doesn't matter," I said, "Hertz, Budget whomever." To which he started laughing, "No," he said. "I mean who are you planning to rent from in Valemount? There are no rental car companies in Valemount."

He kindly towed us to Jasper, where there are many rental car companies.

Erin also had a scary experience driving my Matrix in Edmonton. She slipped off an icy road, went down a hill, and smashed into the side of a lady's car, who was on her way back from her mom's funeral. Fortunately, there were no additional casualties, but if our cars could talk, they would have some interesting tales to tell.

Trains are the Best

Without question, my favourite mode of transport is by train. Unfortunately, in Western Canada, there is very little in the way of availability for passenger train travel. That's a shame, as trains are a far more comfortable mode of transportation than driving or flying. Trains are also a great way to meet people and share stories, particularly if you are traveling a long distance.

As a young person, I took the train across almost the entire country a few times. I was always in coach. I was there because it cost less, but, in retrospect, it also provided me with fuel for many more stories than if I had isolated myself. It's amazing how much you can learn about our country and its inhabitants by travailing with them on the train.

The cross-country train made many stops - some for more than an hour. Most people stayed on board, but I usually ventured out to see what I could see of places I had never been before. I recall multiple stops in northern Ontario where every bar in every town was playing the Kenny Rogers classic, from 1977, "You took a fine time to leave me, Lucille."

In Winnipeg, I wanted to see the famous intersection of Portage and Main. I had never been to Manitoba before but soon discovered that Main Street was not the most tourist-oriented part of the city. I was given an eye-opening introduction to the living conditions of many poor Indigenous people living in the core of many western Canadian cities.

Then, in Saskatchewan, the train made an unscheduled stop in the middle of nowhere and threw off a man who brought his own booze on board.

All the while, it was entertaining just to listen to how people spoke. "Like f...in eh, eh?" was the phrase I most remember. To this day, I have a tendency to pass judgment on people for their language - not so much their swearing but for lazy speech, particularly with the word "*like*" used for no reason.

One of the most interesting conversations heard on the train came when I was a teenager traveling to New Brunswick. I was a huge fan of The Doors, and on this train was their keyboard player, Ray Manzarek. I have no idea why he was traveling by himself by train to New Brunswick, but it sure made for some interesting stories about Jim Morrison and The Doors.

And Finally, Planes

For all the travelling I've done, it is surprising that I have not had multiple encounters with celebrities on the plane. I suspect it is largely because I am not travelling in first-class.

However, we did have a notable exception on the way to L.A. flying from Vancouver. Sitting directly in front of me was one of my favourite musicians, Isaac Hayes, a great black soul singer, and across the aisle from him was the beautiful Jacqueline Smith of Charlie's Angels fame. I was a fan of hers but would not have recognized her with a scarf on her head and large sunglasses, had the flight attendant not spilled the beans. They were flying back to L.A. from a movie shoot in Vancouver.

That would not have made much of a story except that there was construction at L.A.X. Somehow we took a wrong turn and followed the two LA-based celebrities. If one would have assumed they would know their way around L.A.X., one would have been wrong.

Then, once in L.A., we settled into the hotel and were watching The Tonight Show. Host Jay Leno pointed out a guy wearing shorts in the audience and said he must be Canadian as it was unusually cool for Southern California. The next day in the hotel elevator, I saw this guy in shorts and asked him if he had been on The Tonight Show the day before. This guy just glowed. I am sure that he thought he was now a celebrity.

But my favourite plane-related story came on a flight from Vancouver. Actually, it came before the plane even took flight.

I had flown down from Prince George and was taking a flight from Vancouver to somewhere in the U.S. I had the misfortune to be trying to get through security at the same time as a large number of people who had just got off an Alaska cruise ship. By the time we got on the plane, most people were already annoyed with the waiting times. This disposition was only worsened by the lack of air conditioning.

One red neck ahead of me started harping at the female flight attendant, complaining about the lack of air conditioning. She explained that it would get better once the flight started. But he was rude and relentless. Finally, an elderly lady in front of me, told him, "excuse me, sir, I don't like the tone of your voice." To which he replied (to paraphrase Churchill). "That's alright, I don't like the look of your face."

Then in stepped her husband to try and defend his wife. Language escalated, and the rude man was escorted off the plane. Virtually, all the passengers broke into applause, except me.

The lady behind me asked, "Why aren't you applauding? You were right there. You heard how rude he was."

"Absolutely," I said, then asked her if she too didn't find it hot on the plane with no air conditioning. She said, "sure," to which I said, "well, you better get used to it because we are going to be here for another hour while they remove all the luggage from the plane."

Sure enough, once they found and removed his luggage, it was a very uncomfortable hour of sitting in a hot, crowded plane. I am not sure who got the last laugh.

A Few Final Favorite Stories

My favourite one-liner has to be from Winston Churchill. Just for context and for those who don't know it, it went something like this:

"Mr. Churchill, you are drunk."

"Yes, madam, and you are ugly, but I shall be sober tomorrow."

Whether or not he actually said this or how much he was actually responsible for saving the world from the Nazis, he was legendary and would have created lots of chatter on Twitter and other social media.

My next story doesn't quite rank up there in terms of famous quotations, but it has one of my favourite lines.

One summer day a few years ago in Edmonton, I was out doing some weeding just outside the fence we had built. It is one of those metal fences with white strips. I really like that style of the fence as it looks really clean and never needs repair.

While I was there, there was a car parked just beside me with two elderly ladies in it. After a while, I got curious and asked them if they were lost or needed help.

"Not at all," said one. "I used to live in your house. I like what you've done with it, especially the new fence."

She told me her name, and I said that I was still getting mail for a person with that same first name.

She responded, "Oh, that was my husband's name. He was as rotten as the fence you replaced. I got rid of him."

Speaking of memorable responses, here is another one of my family favourites, which I would feel remiss if I didn't include in this epistle.

My dad and I were both born in November, 30 years apart. We also enjoyed friendly competitions - at tennis, table tennis, and, finally, just Scrabble. My dad used to play Scrabble with my mom's mom, and we carried on the tradition with our last game just before he died. I always felt reassured that his mind was still in pretty good shape when he could put together a decent game of Scrabble. And it is something I continue to do with my daughters - although now largely online.

This story began when my dad was 60, and I was 30. We were heading out to play tennis, walking a distance away from their house in Calgary. Before we got to the end of the driveway, my mom hollered out the door for him to be careful to not hurt himself, as he always tried so hard.

I said to him, "You know, dad, mom has a point. I really like playing tennis with you, but you haven't beat me in years. So why not take it a bit easier and just enjoy the game? You are 30 years older than I am."

He responded, "Let's see how you do in 30 years." To which, I said, "But dad, you'll be 90." And he said, "Yah, but you won't be in any shape at 60."

I never forgot that line, and so for my dad's 90th birthday, we had shirts made up with tennis racquets on them, commemorating the tennis challenge - 30 years in the making. His sister Betty and niece Lynda even came out from Ontario to surprise him. Surprise is to put it mildly, as he was virtually in shock to see her.

He looked sharp in his tennis shorts and new shirt. And he fully expected to show off his tennis prowess. However, his showing off pretty much ended with the photo opp, as his body just didn't have the strength and balance anymore, and on one shot, the ball landed on his head - much to his embarrassment. However, I am sure the love and caring shared at this 90th birthday celebration was a memory to be cherished by him and the friends and family who joined us at the court and the surprise party at home that was to follow.

My dad passed away just a month short of his 95th birthday. And I almost died at 62. As people across the world are looking to survive our current COVID-19 Pandemic, I look back at that day and encourage people to make the most of their lives each day.

I hope you have enjoyed my stories. For those who enjoy a game of golf, I am adding a bonus chapter.

CHAPTER FOUR
GOLF STORIES I HAVE KNOWN

Play Smarter, Not Harder

I love to golf but have never been very good at it. "Too much L.O.F.T.," I've been told - "Lack of f...in talent."

Unfortunately, it is one of those sports where focus helps, but too much effort just makes things worse. A little analogy: I had a similar problem with typing in high school. Most of the others in the class could already type and took the class for easy marks. I, being naturally competitive, tried to match their speed. I was fast but made lots of mistakes, for which I was penalized. My typing teacher told my parents that I was "in danger of failing typing in June." They could not understand how I could get such top marks in phys ed but fail typing. Like golf, I eventually got better, but trying too hard (typing or swinging too fast and out of control) was not the key to success. It's a very hard lesson to learn. I still struggle with it. But it is part of what keeps the game challenging.

Years ago, I was playing with the doctors from Prince George Regional Hospital (P.G.R.H.) on their regular weekly outing. I was heading up the hospital foundation at the time, and it was of immense value to get to know the docs, who were so well respected in the community. Plus, it was a great excuse to get in some extra rounds of golf.

Often, some of the pharma reps would join them - I think for pretty much the same reason as I did. What could be better than a day of golf? Plus, they usually paid for drinks afterwards. One of these guys was also a good golfer. In fact, he used to play for a U.S. university golf team that matched up against Stanford and the incredible Tiger Woods (Tiger, of course, was not only amazing in college but carried on to be arguably the best pro golfer of all time). So I asked the pharma rep why he wasn't on the P.G.A. with Tiger. He explained that he wanted to play there more than anything else, but the harder he tried, the worse he played. And so here he was, playing with us in Prince George.

Arnie's Armie

When I worked as a sports reporter at the Edmonton Sun, one of my assignments was to write about what it was like to be part of Arnie's Army since the legendary golf great Arnold Palmer was coming to Edmonton for a golf event. I didn't get to play with him and can't remember if we even spoke, as there were lots of reporters there. I am able to say that I was part of Arnie's Army, but there would be little else to the story, except that I was also invited to play in the pro-am prior to the tournament.

Me, Brad, Henry and Terry at tournament in Kananasakis.

The tournament was at the prestigious, and very private, Mayfair Golf and Country Club. I was in a foursome, which included the president of the Mayfair as well as a pro. I wanted so badly to hit the ball long and hard, but the harder I tried, the worse I sliced. And to make matters worse, they began to patronize me with comments like "that will play" when I had duffed a shot that did not go in the woods. Eventually, I settled down to close to my normal level of mediocrity, but I still finished with my worst score ever - I think it was 117. Arnie never saw me play, but he would not have been impressed.

Another day I really wanted to play well was in the Edmonton sports media tournament. I was fairly new with the Sun and had never played with any of those guys before. Some, like Cam Cole of the Edmonton Journal, were very good golfers, and others were probably not much better than I was. However, I was far more nervous than they were, and the harder I tried, the worse my slice. On one hole, I sliced it off the course, and my ball hit the wheel of a school bus on the adjacent road. Some 40 years have passed since that incident, but when I run into one of those guys, I still sometimes get "How are you doing, Tom? Hit any school buses lately?" I have not been in the business for many years and don't see my former colleagues often. I ran into Cam 10 years ago while attending the 100th Grey Cup in Toronto. We had lots to catch up on, as he had moved on to become a national columnist many years ago. You can guess the first thing he asked me. Some stories just seem to live on forever.

Hitting things that I wasn't supposed to hit has always been a memorable part of my golf game as the next few stories will reflect:

I was part of a weekend foursome playing at Aberdeen Glen, the mountain course in Prince George. We were at an elevated tee box looking way down at the green about 150 yards away. Above us to the left was a row of newly built houses. I said to my golf partner David Wharrie, "There is probably a real estate agent up there telling his clients not to worry because nobody hits the ball up here."

Sure enough, I sliced my seven iron way left (yes, I didn't tell you that I play left-handed). It hit off of the house and down the hill to the edge of the green. After an easy chip and putt, I had my par.

The next morning, I stopped to say hello to one of my Board members (Lynne Fehr), having a coffee. "Were you golfing at Aberdeen on the weekend?" she asked. I affirmed, and she continued, "Oscar (her husband) and I were up there looking at houses when we heard a huge bang. We looked down at the tee, and I told him I think that's Tom."

"And what's more, I got my par," I said.

"And we decided that it was not safe to buy there," she said.

I was out with my buddy Barry Hutchins, playing at Lewis Estates in Edmonton's west end. We came to a long hole with water on the left and trees and houses on the right. Determined not to slice in the water, I pulled a drive into the edge of the trees to my right. I had room to swing my three-wood and hit a rocket that just kept going - across the entire fairway, past the left rough, and over a fence into a backyard. An irate man yelled at me, "You almost hit THE wife." No harm done except for a stroke lost (as Barry and I just count one and move on), and he didn't give me back my ball. I never did see THE wife but wondered why people live right on a golf course if they are not prepared to dodge the odd golf ball.

Two golf seasons ago, I went with Barry out to Wetaskiwin, which was one of four courses in a half-price package (Country Club Tour). We love to play, but neither of us feels good enough about our game to justify putting out 100 bucks a round, once or twice a week. We don't think of ourselves as cheap, and Barry is a very generous guy, but we are cost-conscious. As such, I also cannot resist trying to retrieve my stray golf balls. In this case, I hit one straight and hard, but I was playing my slice/fade. So when it didn't follow my instructions, it went straight at the trees. Naturally, I went looking for it and actually found it, having got through and into a clearing on the other side.

The only problem was that it had also gone off the course and through a barbed-wire fence. I could see it clearly along with three other nice-looking balls, which had suffered the same fate. I knew I could reach them with a club, but in doing so, caught my hand on the fence. Because of my heart event a year or so prior, I am on blood-thinning medication. So my hand bled like crazy. Barry and I searched our golf bags for a band-aid or something to stop the bleeding, which was flowing freely. Fortunately, the kitchen at the clubhouse had some decent band-aids which stemmed the flow. Barry and I teed up again and played the full 18 holes. But I had to promise Barry that I would not try and challenge barbed wire for golf balls ever again.

Barry was also with me at Redtail Landing, a links-style layout near Edmonton International Airport. It's a very challenging course and very hard to find one's ball in the fescue grass. It also has probably the best practice facility in the Edmonton area. We were on the driving range right next to Edmonton Eskimo quarterbacks Rickie Ray and Jason Maas. They had lost to the Lions in B.C. the night before, but it didn't stop them from getting in a round asap on their return.

Maas was not the better quarterback but was by far the better golfer. That day was not that busy, so we were in back-to-back twosomes. It was a great day for Barry and me. I have no idea how we played, but we came home with handfuls of Eskimo logo golf balls, almost all courtesy of Ray, who did not care to look for his stray shots. Fortunately, for the Eskimos, he was much more accurate passing a football than striking a golf ball.

One winter, my friend Orrin Lyseng was talking about heading down to Palm Desert, where he and his brother-in-law Bill, had a triple-wide mobile home. He knew I was interested in going south for the winter, so when he asked if I would like to join him, I jumped at the opportunity. His park included a nine-hole executive golf course, with each hole surrounded by mobile homes. Bill invited his realtor to join our foursome. He also had a mobile home on the site and said he'd be happy to show me around.

When I asked him if the homes got hit often, he assured me "Almost never." I actually got around fine without hitting anything, but Bill put two through windows, including landing one in the kitchen sink of the realtor where his wife was doing the dishes. When we finished, the realtor asked me how I liked it. "I couldn't afford to replace the windows," I replied.

Word to the Wise: If you are having a golf event with your wedding, you might want to think twice about personalized golf balls, especially if there are surrounding condos.

Go Left Young Man, Go Left

I throw left, bat left, and play hockey left, but I started playing golf right-handed. This was not because some golf teacher advised me to play right or that I saw all the right-handed players on T.V. No, the only reason for playing right was that I had to borrow my dad's right-handed clubs. The only left-handed club in my bag was a straight-blade putter (in fact, the oldest club in my bag remains a straight-blade Bullseye putter).

I got used to playing right-handed, but somewhere along the way, I got tired of guys, nowhere near my size or strength, hitting golf balls further than me. I knew I could hit a baseball far harder and further than they could, but that I was doing from the left side - my power side.

One day in Calgary, I got my chance to switch. In a garage sale around the corner from my parents' house, there was a widower selling her late husband's full set of left-handed golf clubs for only $35, complete with the Spalding box they came in. How could I pass them by?

That was about 40 years ago, and although I have changed clubs a few times, I have never changed back to playing right-handed (except for the odd shot on the driving range or under a tree), and then I wonder how I ever swung that way. It's amazing how awkward it can be to change the way you have been doing something, even if it is reverting back to a past method.

I have had a number of drivers and woods, but I am only on my fourth set of left-handed irons. Ironically, my garage sale set was stolen from my garage, the day we moved into our home in Lansdowne in south Edmonton. However, I have to thank that thief as my insurance policy called for a replacement. I was able to buy a new set of mid-level Spalding clubs. I used them for many years before purchasing a set of used Lynx irons from my nephew Scott.

Unfortunately, one day I broke the seven iron from the Lynx set and could not find a decent replacement. I have had a few clubs snap on me over the years but usually woods, which are easily (although perhaps not cheaply) replaced. But replacing an iron from a set that is no longer being made is much more difficult. And the seven-iron is probably the worst to go as it was my go-to iron. With an average hit, it went about 150 yards - and with 150-yard markers on every course, I often used them as a target to give me a consistent distance to the hole.

So, after purchasing about three unsatisfactory seven irons, I gave in and purchased a new mini-set of irons (5-PW) from a Christmas golf *"garage sale"* put on by several local clubs. When I was young, my favourite club was a two-iron, but now, with some nice hybrids in my bag, I seldom carry anything longer than a five. I am quite sure that one's game would improve much more with lessons and practice than with new clubs, but who wants to go that route when you can buy instant success with new clubs.

However, perhaps my most dramatic and comedic breaking of a club wasn't even mine. I had bought my dad a new driver for Father's Day and was demonstrating its use on our front lawn in Toronto, with both my dad and my friend Frank watching from the step. However, the club never had a chance to perform as I hit a telephone pole cable with my backswing, snapping it in half. "Happy Father's Day... sorry about that, Pops."

My first hybrid-style club was a Heaven Wood from Callaway. It had the face of a seven wood but the length of a four. It quickly became my go-to fairway wood for shots to the green as, in the day, I could hit it between 180 - 200 yards, and it would land softly (sadly, now it carries only 150 - 160 yards, no further than I used to hit a seven iron). The club was special in part because my buddy Brad Gifford bought it for me for shoveling his and his sister's driveways when they were in Florida. They had large driveways, and it snowed a lot, so I really felt I earned that club, even if Brad claims that my shoveling reduced his driveway from a double to a single.

Golf Courses

Golf is very sticky (stodgy) about the rules which, except for some local rules, apply everywhere you play. It is one of the things that people either love or hate most about the sport.

However, unlike most other sports where your arena, gym, field, or court are standard, golf courses vary incredibly.

One of the most unique courses is in Yellowknife, Northwest Territories. I was there to help my friend Dennis Cleaver, who was C.E.O. of their hospital, with the training of a relatively new Foundation Board. Dennis had been C.E.O. at P.G.R.H. when I was hired to come to run its Foundation, and I was happy to help - and to see Yellowknife.

I also wanted to get in a round of golf while I was there, as I had heard about their annual 24-hour tournament. I was there in September, so daylight was scarce, but I soon discovered that the length of day was not the only peculiarity there. Trees grew no taller than my height (roughly six feet), and grass barely grew at all. The greens were artificial, and the only grass growing on the course was in the chipping area around the greens.

Players carried with them a piece of artificial turf, which they used for all shots off the ground until one reached the green area. Having played off desert conditions in the Phoenix area, I was not all that concerned about playing off the rough surface - and so I was not troubled when I left my piece of carpet on one of the holes. However, I soon found out that the carpet was more valuable than any club in my bag, and the guys I were playing with became tired of lending me theirs. I will know better next time and put an extra piece of carpet in my bag.

For pretty much opposite conditions to Yellowknife, I would suggest giving golfing a go in Prince Rupert. Not only is it one of the rainiest areas you can find but the course is also built on reclaimed land of some sort. Here, when you hit your ball, you don't have to worry about losing it in fescue or wrecking your clubs on hard ground - your challenge is finding your ball if hit perfectly and coming straight down. Balls bury themselves in the wet ground, such that you are lucky if you can even see the top of the ball when standing right over it. Playing it where it lies is usually a fun challenge, but on this course, it is sometimes impossible without a drilling kit. I played with three other "Dance Dads" there to watch our daughters compete in the annual Prince Rupert Dance Festival. We had a great time, with local conditions only adding to the fun - and stories to be told of the perfect shot that was never found.

Golf courses are some of the most scenic sites in the world, whether it be the sand dunes and red sands in P.E.I., ocean views from the coast, or the spectacular Rocky Mountains in Alberta and B.C.

I love to get in a round at Banff, Kananaskis, or Jasper as the scenery and wildlife are as good as it gets. One time, I was fortunate to play Jasper during a weekday with a couple of friends. It was early afternoon in the late spring, and we were joined by a local looking to pick up a game. As is normally the case in such circumstances, I asked him what he did for a living. He said, "I'm a school teacher." I looked at my watch and commented, "I know that schools get out earlier now than in my day, but this (about 1:30) is really early." He responded, "oh, I don't work full-time. Nobody moves to Jasper to work full-time. My wife is a part-time nurse, and she doesn't even answer the phone if she doesn't feel like working." I learned a lesson that day - not about golfing, but choosing a location to fit your lifestyle.

I also learned at Jasper that we were only visitors on the land on which we played - and I am not talking about Indigenous golfers. As it turns out, the elk that you see so often in town and on the roads leading in also like the surroundings on the golf course.

On one hole, which was all downhill towards the green, I hit my approach shot towards an elk to the right of the green. I went down to play my chip shot, but my golf buddies yelled at me to get the hell out of there. I looked up and saw the elk with its head down, getting ready to charge. It could care less about my shot, but I had cut off its route to escape and, with a Texas gate on the ground on the other side of the green, it had nowhere to go but through me.

I had a similar experience in Florida but with a much different animal. I picked up a game with a couple of guys near Tampa. It was a typical Florida course with water on almost every hole. I hit a shot near a large water hazard and was getting ready to chip when the guys told me to forget about the shot and get away from the hazard. Apparently, the gator living there did not take kindly to intruders.

Apparently, in Mackenzie, a forestry town north of Prince George, the problem was with an even more threatening animal - the grizzly bear. The town was getting complaints about grizzlies at the garbage dump, so they put up an electric fence. So, the grizzlies migrated to the golf course. One spring day, I played there and complained to the marshall about the snow still on parts of the course. He said I was lucky as about the time the snow was gone, the grizzlies came out. It would give social distancing a new meaning.

In Panama, the animal gracing us was a huge, beautiful iguana. It lay on the green and posed for pictures with not a care about me or my putt. Harmony.

In Puerto Vallarta, I did not take my clubs on a family holiday but did try out miniature golf - a free attraction in the back of the restaurant where we were going for breakfast. However, blocking one of the holes was a huge, dead rat. I went in to tell the restaurant owner, as I didn't think a dead rat was good for business for a restaurant. With my poor Spanish and her lack of English, it took a while and a little charades to explain, but once she understood, she said something high pitched in Spanish and went out with her broom to remove the rat... We were hungry, so we still went in for breakfast. The eggs and tortillas were great, rat or no rat.

Atlantic Adventures

My best, and certainly funniest, golf trip ever was with my brother Jamie, from Calgary, and my friend Frank Cairns, with whom I have golfed since our high school days in Toronto. Jamie is six and a half years my junior, and I left for university at 17, so the two really did not know each other as middle-aged adults. However, somehow we decided to go on a golf trip together through the Maritimes and across Newfoundland. Both Jamie and Frank are great storytellers, often with the added colour of various, perhaps not politically correct, accents. Unfortunately, I can't capture the accents here, so I hope these stories are not lost in the telling. However, I can say that it was not just me who was laughing loudly, but others who were attracted to the conversation, including a couple from Chicago. They were at the table next to us at dinner in P.E.I. and laughed so hard that they actually met us on the green of the course we were playing the next day, just to enjoy more stories at the 19th hole.

One of our most memorable days was in New Brunswick, where we played the Algonquin Golf Course in the lovely fishing village of St. Andrew's By The Sea. Farrah, who was my brother's tenant in Saint John, booked the time through a friend of hers - a golf pro at the club. She shared a cart with me and a supply of port and beer in the other cart.

Farrah had dated this pro and obviously picked up a few tips as she had a much better swing than us. However, I thought I could give her a suggestion to play even better. I said, "You have a nice swing. But I think if you could get your hips better through the ball, you would hit it even further."

I actually meant it seriously, but she somehow took it as a shot at the width of her hips - and slugged me. Jamie and Frank still tell the story - and probably better than I have here.

After finishing off most of the beer and port (Frank's drink of choice) and Jamie driving all over the golf course with his cart, we went into town for dinner. There were all sorts of great places to eat and we, of course, chose seafood (warning: Don't ever ask Jamie to explain the New Jersey Devils' trap system, especially when he's been drinking and only has the salt and pepper shakers and vinegar there to demonstrate).

When we got back to the house that Jamie and I owned in Chance Harbour, we were greeted by my cousin Stephen's wife, Sharon, who lived about 50 yards up the hill.

"You boys been in the drink, have you?" she said. "Stephen's been waiting for you."

So we walked up the hill to see Stephen. "Where ya bin?" he asked in his distinct Maritime drawl. I answered, "We were golfing in St. Andrew's and stayed there for dinner."

He responded in all seriousness, "Well, I cooked up lobster supper for youse," to which we said, "Did you not think to let us know?"

"Yaaaah," he said. Stephen has since passed, but our memories of him will never die. And I couldn't resist telling the longer version of this story.

As a side note: On another trip back there, this time accompanied by my wife Sheila and Frank's wife Corinne, we did plan a big lobster meal. We built a fire down on the rocky beach nearby, with the tides from the Bay of Fundy coming in. We ordered about two dozen lobster from Stephen, but only about six of us were able to make it, and only four ate lobster. We also forgot to request tools and ended up breaking the lobsters with rocks. We returned that night to Jamie's house in Saint John with too many lobsters to eat before we were to fly out. So the next day, when a couple of students came to his door on behalf of an international foster parents charity, Jamie agreed to sponsor a child, but only if the students would each take a lobster home with them. It was a story not only for us to remember, but I am sure a new experience for the students as well - and a good day for some needy child in Africa.

The second province to visit was golf-rich P.E.I. It has probably more great golf courses per square mile than anywhere else in Canada, and with the Confederation Bridge now allowing visits by car, it has transformed into a summer tourist Mecca. I particularly enjoyed Crowbush Cove, with its beautiful sand dunes and seaside views. However, on the day we played, the wind was blowing hard off the dunes, and it seemed like every shot was into at least a three-club wind. I opted to walk the course but, after about 14 holes, was exhausted, and it was all I could do to finish. Golf in the Maritimes is beautiful, but you never know what you are going to get for weather.

This uncertainty was most evident in our lost stop on our tour, which was to be the Highlands golf course on Cape Breton - one of the top-ranked courses in North America. But we never saw it. We arrived in the dark and pouring rain. And the next day, the fog was so thick that we couldn't even see the course, let alone play it. Fortunately, the people at the bed and breakfast were tremendous hosts, and so all was not lost.

Last but not least of the provinces was Newfoundland. We took the ferry to Port Aux Basques on the west end of the Rock. The trip was more than six hours but aside from Jamie turning greener than the ocean from motion sickness, it was uneventful. We were thankful to arrive at our bed and breakfast, ready to retire early.

However, little did we know that the lady of the house had been waiting for the boys from the mainland... largely for us to keep her husband company. We were dead tired but agreed to watch the Blue Jays game with him.

We asked him what he had done for a living, and he told us that he was an engineer and "Drove the train from coast to coast." So, half-asleep, I said, "All the way to Victoria?" He responded, "No, across Newfoundland, laddie." I had not only neglected that Newfoundland was an island, but that crossing to Victoria would have been a fun challenge as well. At least, we left him with a good tale to tell the next visitors to the Rock.

We rented a car, played my Stan Rogers CDs and continued driving to the little village of Stephensville, where we booked a round of golf. The course marshal asked if we would mind if he added one of the locals to our foursome. Jimmy was well into his 80s and proudly told us that he was the oldest member of the course. "You boys hit a long ball," he told us several times and kindly accepted our offer of another beer. Along the way, I asked him if he was married. He said, "No, I'm not married. Hilda's been chasing me for the past 17 years or so, but she ain't gonna catch me."

Jimmy joined us for a few more drinks after the round and, by the time we left, I think that he had introduced his new friends to every member of the Stephensville golf club.

We later carried on to St. John's to visit Alex Faseruk, a good friend of mine and Frank's, who was a business professor at Memorial University. As Alex is not a golfer, I will save my Alex stories for another day except to say that the one round we played with him was memorable not for the golf, but rather the exploding golf ball that Frank had bought for Alex. It worked perfectly and caught Alex totally by surprise. He was still a great host in a great place.

It's a shame that it is such a long and expensive trip to get to the Maritimes (and especially Newfoundland) from Western Canada. It is a tremendous area of the country to visit, and you are sure to come back with some of your best golf stories - even when you don't play.

Golf Buddies

You will notice that most of my stories include my friends/golf buddies. There is a good reason for this. As much as I enjoy the game, a major part of it is spending that time with friends. In fact, I seldom play with strangers and have few good friends who don't play - including some I take some credit for either introducing them to the game, or (and more often) reviving their interest in it.

One of the people whom I most admire for joining me was Gilad, then my daughter Erin's boyfriend from Israel. As if meeting your future father-in-law for the first time after flying umpteen hours to get here was not enough cause for stress, he had never even held a golf club before. Plus, he was joining me at my favourite sport and playing indoors at that. I think he put 10 balls in the virtual water on one hole, but he did not give up or complain. He won me over with his attitude. They are now very happily married, and he has never given me reason to not like him or not trust him with my daughter. Seldom has golf misled me in a measure of men. Unfortunately, there are only two golf courses in all of Israel, so Gilad doesn't have that much opportunity to practice his game for when I come to visit.

Where's Jamie?

I was fortunate to be asked to join a bunch of guys from Prince George on a golf trip into the Okanagan and Shushwap. They even had room for Jamie to come up from Calgary to join us. One of the most anticipated stops was at Predator Ridge, near Vernon. It is a beautiful course but was, at the time, still new with a lot of construction taking place. After the round, Jamie was annoyed by the noise and went in to complain to the pro shop.

Edmonton golf buddies Barry, Steve and Doug join me for a CMHA charity tourney.

I was in the lead car and Jamie in the second car, which, of course, included the beer. After the round, our car left, assuming that Jamie, an engineer, would stay with the beer. However, the beer car also left, assuming Jamie would be driving with his brother. Before the time of cell phones, it wasn't until we stopped about an hour later that we realized that we had left Jamie back at the course. At least he had managed to talk the course into discounting our green fees.

That trip I also remember playing in a foursome with my former Board chair and friend (since deceased), Del Laverdure. We were on the green, and I was facing a mid-length putt. However, it was in shadow, so I asked Del to move. The only problem was that it was my shadow. Needless to say, the needles were out after that one - as they were when my ball landed in an area full of manure. "Play it where it lies," said Del. He too died too young, and I miss him.

Golf for a Lifetime

I have played a lot of sports in my 65 years, and I am quite sure that golf is nowhere near the top of my list in terms of skills or achievement. However, it has brought me the most enjoyment and the fewest injuries of any sport that I have taken on somewhat seriously.

Aside from some straining of muscles, the only injuries that I have sustained or caused in golf were from the golf ball, which is hard, moves fast, and is often unpredictable as to where it is going.

In that regard, Jamie is even more dangerous than I am, as he hits the ball harder and with even less control than I have as to where it goes.

One day, I was playing in a company golf tournament with him at Kananaskis, which has the most beautiful white sand bunkers anywhere in Canada (and has discounted fees for Albertans). Getting out of bunkers looks simple when you watch the pros, but is anything but for me - or Jamie. Just a few holes in, he hit one in a fairway bunker, and I decided to capture his exit with the 35 mm Nikon that I had brought just for such an occasion. I set up to the side of the trap and caught the ball perfectly coming out of the sand. Unfortunately, it was coming right at me and struck off my front elbow, which was in front of me holding up the camera. Once the film was developed, the resulting photo showed a golf ball looking the size of a softball. And it was not long before the swelling on my elbow looked like I had a golf ball attached. Jamie, naturally, blamed me for blocking his shot.

I can only remember hitting one person myself. I was playing with the docs from PGRH. I had trouble finding my first shot so my group went ahead. I found my ball near the trees and drilled my second shot right at one of the specialists - a friend named Dr. Clark Jamieson. He was well down the fairway and near the woods on the other side. He heard me yell when I hit it but caught a tree root, which turned his back to the oncoming ball, which hit him squarely. Over drinks afterwards, he didn't complain about my taking the shot but that it had tightened up his back and ruined what was going to be a good game (in checking the spelling of his name, I see that Clark died a few years ago. He was just an average golfer, but a fine doctor and a great guy).

The Sweet Spot

I haven't spoken that much so far about actual golf shots - in particular, good ones. But as every golfer knows, there is no better feeling than hitting the sweet spot with your swing. For players like me, that feeling only comes two or three times a game. But it keeps you coming back, whether it be a drive, approach shot, or a putt.

As I have described, when I was younger (and prior to my heart event on February 26, 2017), my swing was much faster, but also wilder. I was able, at times, to hit the ball 300 yards; therefore, if I hit the ball well, I could reach most par fives in two (but that's a big if) and even reached some short Par fours with my drive. I am also a good putter, so I was able to register the odd eagle. However, since I have lost that distance and am less wild, I am eagle-less, but my scores are actually no higher now than they were then. As my high school math teacher once told me, "What you gain in the bananas you lose in the peaches." I wasn't much of a math student, but this also seems to apply to golf, which is one of the reasons people can still enjoy the game as they get older. I used to marvel at the old guys still playing, but now that I am one of them, I can't see any reason to stop.

I have never seen a hole in one, let alone score one. My closest was a shot in a Rotary tournament in Prince George that ended up four and a half inches from the hole. I put my name and distance from the hole on the card there, right underneath another guy whose shot was one and a half feet away. I thought it was too bad for him, but I won the K.P. However, it turned out that his shot was only one and a half inches away. The tournament organizers felt my pain and gave me a sleeve of balls as a consolation.

Perhaps the strangest sequence of shots that I can remember was at the P.G. Golf and Curling Club where I was a member for several years. I loved having the membership, which was donated to my workplace, and played two or three times a week, once with the docs and often with my golf buddies Dave Wharrie and Graham Holmes. We often played early in the morning on weekends before any booked time and while the ground keepers were still out preparing the course. The rounds were done quickly, but by the time we finished breakfast and several coffee refills, we had taken up most of the morning.

On one outing, we had just finished a par five and were on the following par three. As we were about to tee off, I looked around and saw a guy in the group behind us sink his second shot on the part 5 from well over 200 yards away - a rare albatross. I messed up my tee shot, hitting it off to the right and into the trees. Not wanting to hold things up, I went to look for it while my partners teed off. Graham hit his shot equally as poorly, only to the left side. However, it hit off a tree and angled across the fairway and right into my bag, which I was pulling on a pull cart. I figured the odds of that shot with those angles had to be about as high as that of the albatross just before it. Graham just said, "The least you could have done is carry it with you down to the green."

Every year, my hospital Foundation held a Pro-Am golf tournament with three amateurs and one club pro (from B.C. and Alberta) playing his or her own ball. The pros enjoyed the chance to get away from teaching lessons at their home clubs and getting together with each other, and some appreciative amateurs. One year, our pro had a long putter, which was not behaving for him. By about our 14th hole after missing yet another putt, he hurled his expensive putter into the pond and putted the rest of the round with his three wood. One of my friends asked me what I thought when our pro literally threw away our chances. I said. "he putted better with this three wood. If I had known that, I would have thrown away his putter much earlier in the round." Later, somebody put on a wet-suit and goggles and retrieved the putter, although I'm not sure our pro ever made peace with it. Too bad it was not left-handed.

I am going to save one of my favourite stories to last.

As you can see by the cover page, my surname is Shand. It is a very simple Scottish name, which sounds as straightforward as it looks. Aside from my dad mistaking calls on the office intercom for "Dick Chan," I can't recall many cases of mistaken identity in pronouncing Shand.

However, one day I was out with Barry and my brother-in-law Steve Harrison and a fourth whom I can't recall. I had booked the tee time, so the announcement from the clubhouse came in my name... "At the tee, the Shuh - hand" foursome. "Have you joined the Taliban?" asked Steve. The first tee is usually a little tense, but this time everybody was loosened up, even your author, Tom Shuh-hand.

I hope you have enjoyed reading these stories as much as I have enjoyed recalling them. Special thanks go out to my golf buddies from over the years, for your friendship, tolerance, and shared love of golf. A sincere note of appreciation also goes out to my wife Sheila for not begrudging me the time, or costs, to play, and sometimes even joining me. It's a great game, and I do so love to play. I hope to join for a round some day.

Editor's Note - The day is June 22, 2020. Ten days ago, the Alberta Government introduced Phase II of the province's Relaunch strategy following widespread testing (389,405 tests to date) and low rates of infection. With the new stage comes the re-openings of gyms, movie theatres, recreational sports, and other staples of life pre-COVID. The question remains whether these facilities will contribute to a second wave of the disease, rendering the province a victim of its own success.

So far, the results have inspired cautious optimism. As expected, the infection rate in the province has risen since the commencement of the relaunch plan. There are currently 534 active cases - still considerably less than the province's peak of 2,992 cases on April 30. From June 13 to 21, 152 people recovered while 251 new cases were confirmed. For the first time, Edmonton outpaces Calgary in terms of infection. The latter city had previously been Alberta's most prevalent site of infection.

In total, 152 Albertans have died from COVID-19 to date.

www.ingramcontent.com/pod-product-compliance
Lightning Source LLC
Chambersburg PA
CBHW030120170426
43198CB00009B/681